Chinese
Myths

Eras

Antiquity:	*c.* 2000 BC to AD 300
Medieval era:	*c.* AD 300 to 1600
Pre-modern era:	*c.* 1600 to 1850
Modern era:	*c.* 1850 to present

Chronology of ancient China

Late Palaeolithic	16,922 BC
Neolithic	*c.* 5500–2000 BC
Shang	?1766–?1123 BC
Zhou	?1123–221 BC
Han	221 BC–AD 220

Note on pronunciation

For the transliteration of Chinese names and terms the Pinyin system has been used throughout, except for the familiar spelling of the Yangtze River (Yangzi in Pinyin) and some original illustration captions.

Mostly the sounds of the Pinyin transliteration are the same as for English, but the following differences should be noted:

Can is pronounced Tsan			Si	:	Sser
Ce	:	Tser	Xie	:	Shieh
Di	:	Dee	Xu	:	Shu
E	:	Er	Yi	:	Ee
He	:	Her	You	:	Yo
Qi	:	Chee	Yu	:	You
Qun	:	Chyun	Zhuan	:	Juan
Shi	:	Sher	Zi	:	Dzer

THE · LEGENDARY · PAST

Chinese

Myths

ANNE BIRRELL

Published in co-operation with
BRITISH MUSEUM PRESS
UNIVERSITY OF TEXAS PRESS, AUSTIN

First University of Texas Press edition, 2000

ISBN 0-292-70879-3
Library of Congress Catalog Card Number 00-039296

Requests for permission to reproduce material from this work should be sent to
Permissions, University of Texas Press, Box 7819, Austin, TX 78713-7819

Designed by Martin Richards
Cover design by Slatter-Anderson
Set in 10 $^{1}/_{2}$ pt Sabon by Wyvern 21, Bristol
Printed in Great Britain by The Bath Press, Avon

This page: The Great Wall (photo courtesy of Anne King).

*Front cover: Gilt-bronze dragon head, probably a handle for a lacquer vessel,
dating to the Western Han dynasty (2nd–1st century BC). Length 14.5 cm.
Private collection. Photo © The British Museum.*

Contents

Introduction

The mythology of Chinese culture and civilization is contained in a variety of sacred narratives which tell how the world and human society were created in their present form. They are sacred narratives because they relate acts of the deities in addition to other episodes, and they embody the most deeply felt spiritual values of a nation. A generally accepted Western definition of myth as 'sacred narrative' reflects the meaning of the Chinese term for myth, *shen-hua*: *shen* means 'divine, deity, holy'; *hua* means 'speech, tale, oral narrative'. The concerns of myth also extend beyond the accounts of the deities, including stories about world catastrophes of flood, fire, drought, famine, of eating, exile and migration, besides leadership qualities, human government, the hero figure and the foundation of dynasties, peoples and clans.

The modern study of mythology combines the disciplines of anthropology, the classics, comparative religion, history, folklore, literature, art and psychology. This broader line of inquiry into the nature of myth contrasts with the study of myth in the nineteenth century, which centred more narrowly on questions of origins and the idea of myth as an explanation of primitive science and primitive society. Compared with the study of Western mythologies, especially those of Greece and Rome, the study of Chinese myth is still in its infancy. Initially, the study of Chinese myth was heavily influenced by the origins and explanations, or 'etiological', approach. But it is now opening up to more contemporary theories of comparative mythology and the worldwide study of mythology, so Chinese mythology is proving to be a valuable and exciting treasure trove of mythic themes, motifs and archetypes.

The subjects and concerns of Chinese mythology can be traced back to the cultural and environmental factors which shaped the earliest form of Chinese civilization in antiquity. The beginnings of this civilization are inextricably linked to its favourable environment. Three zones of ecogeographical systems developed in the land mass of China. There is the temperate North China belt with its fertile plains alluviated by the Yellow River. Its seed culture of millet and hemp, mulberry and fruit trees, and grasslands were conducive to the evolution of wild and domestic plants and animals, and to human habitation. But this region was also prone to harsh winters, severe droughts and catastrophic floods. The South China belt forms a second zone, with a stable, mild and humid climate, the region being alluviated by the Yangtze River. Its vegetative propagation culture benefits from an all-year growing season. It is an aquatic agricultural system that is favourable to rice, beans, lotus, bamboo, fish and turtles. The third zone is the Deep South China belt with rich coastal fishing grounds and a tropical ecosystem.

The different but equally favourable environments of north and south contributed to the dual origin of human culture in China, and led to the emergence of numerous communities of similar economic levels but with varying cultural systems. The earliest known sites of human habitation are the Neolithic settlements at Banpo in the Wei River valley in the north (near modern Xi'an, Shaanxi province) and Hemudu in the Yangtze River valley in the south-east (Zhejiang province). These centres of village farming are datable to around 5000 BC for Banpo and (by radiocarbon techniques) 3718 BC for Hemudu.

The environmental factors of climate, terrain, vegetation, animal life, mineral resources and topology contributed to the gradual evolution of diverse food-producing communities in the major river valleys of the Yellow (Huang) River, the Wei and Han Rivers in the north, the Huai River in the central region, and the Yangtze River in the south.

The development of Chinese civilization must also be viewed from the perspective of its ancient borders and its neighbouring countries in antiquity. China was to some extent protected by natural barriers. It was bounded to the north by the Gobi desert, to the west by the Kunlun and Himalayan mountains, to the east and south-east by the sea. This geographic cordon ensured that embryonic Chinese settlements were neither systematically eliminated nor repeatedly invaded by neighbouring peoples. On the other hand, the geographic disposition of its borders allowed for corridors and routes of communication which facilitated cultural diffusion. Modern research is still in the process of determining which cultural inventions are indigenous to China and which were the result of cultural diffusion. It is believed that millet, the staple crop of north China, arrived from fertile oases in Central Asia, and that rice originated in India and arrived in China by a land route of transfusion through south-east Asia. The cultural innovations of a writing system and metallurgy that were successfully exploited by the rulers of the earliest Chinese state may have been transmitted from non-Chinese peoples rather than independently invented by the ancient Chinese. Other cultural influences are discernible from Siberia in the north, Melanesia in the south-east, Tibet in the south-west, and most crucially from Central Asia in the west through the Tarim Basin, whose peoples formed points of contact with the Middle East and Near East.

The ambiguous relationship between the relative insularity of the Chinese land mass and the proximity of neighbouring ethnic peoples raises the question of the origins of the Chinese people. Considering the size and importance of the region, firm evidence is remarkably poor for their physical origin. The major discovery of skeletal remains in a cave at Zhoukoutian near Beijing, which has been radiocarbon-dated to 16,922 BC, were initially classified as Peking Man hominids but are now believed to be related to American Plains Indians rather than Asiatic or Mongoloid types. The earliest Mongoloid skeleton was found in south China, in Guangxi province, though its date and identification are indefinite. Identification is insecure for an incomplete skull from Sichuan province dated at 5535 BC. One authoritative view is that the origins of the Chinese derive from Mongoloids who represent a mixture of racial populations of great antiquity, which are as diverse as Polynesians and American Indians. But the evidence for the ancestry of the people inhabiting the land mass of China between 10,000 and 5000 BC awaits further archaeological research.

Coming to the Neolithic period, skeletal remains from village cemeteries

Shang dynasty bronze axe decorated with the gaping mouth of a monstrous demon.

of north China dating from around 5000 BC show Mongoloid features with no significant ethnic diversity. For the later period of antiquity, the Late Shang era *c.* 1200 BC, data from sacrificial pits show a great diversity of racial origin, including Melanesian, Eskimo and Caucasoid types. But the ethnic origins of people buried in sacrificial pits, who were presumably non-Chinese prisoners of war, may be separated from the ethnic identity of the emergent civilization in China during the late second to early first millennia BC. Current scholarly findings lead to some firm conclusions. First, the Neolithic northern population shows a considerable physical homogeneity. Second, the population of north China has remained surprisingly homogeneous since the Neolithic era (*c.* 5550–*c.* 2000 BC). Third, the data point to the lack of any significant migration to or foreign invasion of the region during and since around 5000 BC.

Of the three ecogeographical systems in the land mass of China, the North China belt proved to be the most favourable for the development of China's first state and for the beginnings of Chinese civilization. Early on, its culture expanded to take the form of numerous ethnic communities distributed along the main river valleys of the Yellow, Wei, Han, Huai and Yangtze rivers. Their traits were equally developed by the Neolithic era. One of these ethnic groups emerged by about 1700 BC as the dominant power in the Yellow River region of the Central Plains. It progressed to become the first Chinese dynasty, the Shang, with a major site of power in Anyang city (modern Henan province). Two separate Neolithic northern cultures have been

Bronze vessel, gui, *of the late 11th century* BC.

identified by their pottery styles: the Yangshao culture of painted pottery developed along the Central Plains region of the Yellow River, while the Longshan culture of unpainted black pottery was distributed over a large area to the south and east. The Shang state took its genesis from the Longshan culture of Henan province. It rose to prominence in an era of unprecedented cultural and technological innovation. The success of the Shang was due to its superior system of military organization, control of food production, urban settlements, institutions of kinship and the priesthood, methods of transport and communication, and its distinctively robust artistic expression. The Shang state had the power and authority to organize the construction of impressive buildings and to attract specialists such as record-keepers, soldiers, retainers and artisans to maintain the state apparatus and to conduct large-scale ritual ceremonies, including human sacrifice in the burial rite of the ruling elite.

Two factors played a crucial role in the rise of the Shang state and the beginnings of Chinese civilization. Technological expertise in bronze metallurgy meant supremacy in war and material culture. The invention of a usable writing system consisting of graphs or characters by around 1200 BC led to improved methods of social organization through the bureaucratic and administrative control of commerce, calendrical regulation of agriculture, foreign affairs, alliances and religious practices.

Central to the identity and function of the state was the Shang concept of a priestly king. The king's functions were to make divination to the royal

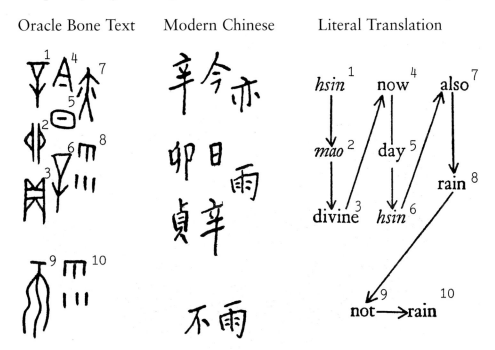

Translation of an oracle bone inscription: 'On this xin-mao *day we divine whether today,* xin (hsin), *it will rain or will not rain'.*

ancestors, to conduct rituals in honour of the ancestors, to make a sacred and symbolic progress through Shang territory, to hold audience, to bestow honours, to lead in war, and to lead the royal hunt. The king's was an itinerant power, as there was no fixed Shang capital. Instead there were several sites that served as ritual, technological and funerary centres. The king ruled through the intercession of the great god Di (pronounced Dee).

One of the north-west regions visited by Shang kings was the Wei River valley west of the Yellow River, which was inhabited by the Zhou people. The Zhou belonged to a different ethnic group from the Shang, but they absorbed Shang cultural influences. They were a warrior people and in time they conquered their Shang overlords and established the Zhou dynasty *c.* 1123 BC. Zhou society was organized into strictly defined social classes and functions, with a dual emphasis on warfare and agricultural productivity. The Zhou kings embarked on a military strategy to unite the diverse communities of the north and south, extending their power into what is now Manchuria and Inner Mongolia, and to the regions north and south of the Yangtze River. They reorganized these settlements into a loose federation of kingdoms (*guo*) to form the Zhou state. Military expansion was reinforced by a hierarchy of aristocratic warriors and a food-producing peasantry who supplied conscript service and forced labour.

The Zhou introduced moral rigour to their political and social system, echoes of which are to be found in China's first literary work, the Zhou *Classic of Poetry* of around 600 BC. The Zhou abandoned the great god Di of the Shang, and instead they worshipped the sky god Tian, with the Zhou king designated as Son of the Sky God (Tian Zi). Zhou divination methods included the use of milfoil or yarrow stalks, culminating in the Zhou text *Classic of Change* (*Yi jing*, pronounced E jing).

The Zhou political system flourished for several centuries but by the fourth century BC it had begun to disintegrate. As early as the year 771 BC Zhou power was effectively diminished, and the capital was moved east from Xi'an to Luoyang, but the king retained nominal control over the federation of kingdoms. These kingdoms gradually formed independent centres of political, military and economic power. They began to merge into larger polities that in the Warring States era of the fifth to third centuries BC contended for supremacy over a reunited state. The most militaristic of these kingdoms, the Qin of Shaanxi province in the north-west, successfully unified the residual Zhou kingdoms into the first Chinese empire. Though short-lived (only sixteen years of rule), it was followed by the four-centuries-long Han empire, which continued Qin socio-economic policies and consolidated imperial power.

Although the Shang had developed a writing system, its main function was divination by the priesthood and later by the king alone. Thousands of inscriptions found at Anyang city consist of oracle bones. The Shang script was not used to record their origins, myths or sacred history. The disintegration of the Zhou empire in the fourth century BC led to cultural fragmentation and the dispersal of older value-systems. Hence the perceived need for classical writers to record and preserve for posterity the remembered heritage

☰ Qian	Heaven	☵ Kan	Water, Moon
☷ Kun	Earth	☲ Li	Fire, Sun
☳ Zhen	Thunder	☶ Gen	Mountain
☴ Sun	Wood, Rain	☱ Dui	Marsh

The great god Fu Xi invents the hexagrams of the Yi jing.

of their sacred history. Since their different versions of the myths are relatively consistent, it must be assumed that these writers were drawing on a communal fund of oral traditions that date from before the first recorded myths in China's earliest text, the *Classic of Poetry*. Very few recognizably Shang or Zhou myths survive. Most recorded myth is undatable and takes its ancestry from the date of the written texts that were themselves based on an archaic oral tradition.

The myths of ancient China that emerged from the oral tradition were preserved in classical texts during the Age of the Philosophers with the advent of literary texts in the sixth to third centuries BC. The decline of the Zhou coincided with the emergence of great thinkers and writers, such as Confucius and Mencius of the Confucian school and Zhuang Zhou of the Daoist school. Ancient China had no Hesiod, Homer or Ovid to retell the mythic oral tales at length. Instead, Chinese writers introduced fragmentary passages of mythic stories into their works of philosophy and history to illustrate their arguments and give authority to their statements. Chinese myth thus exists as an amorphous, diffuse variety of anonymous archaic expression that is preserved in the contexts of philosophical, literary and historical writings. They are brief, disjointed and enigmatic. These mythic fragments incorporated into miscellaneous classical texts vary in their narration, and authors often adapted myth according to their own point of view. The result is that Chinese myth survives in numerous versions, the content of which is broadly consistent, but which shows significant variation in the details. Whereas the reshaping of archaic oral Greek and Roman myths into an artistic form of narrative literature implies the loss of the authentic oral voice, the Chinese method of recording mythic fragments in a wealth of untidy, variable stories is a rare survival of primitive authenticity.

The themes of Chinese myths have significant parallels with those of other world mythologies. Where they diverge is in their central concern and cultural distinctiveness. Major mythic themes are narrated in several versions, such as the six story lines of the creation of the world and the four flood myth stories. The world picture of one Chinese creation myth shows similarities with ancient Egyptian cosmology. Other creation myths in the Chinese tradition contrast with the Biblical and other versions in their lack of a divine cause or a creator. One major creation myth, the myth of the cosmological human body, has features similar to ancient Iranian mythology. Chinese flood myths are unique for the absence of the motif of divine retribution and of divine intervention in halting the deluge. Instead, the central concern of the major Chinese flood myth focuses on the concept of human control of the catastrophe through the moral qualities of the warrior hero. Drought myth, probably deriving from the arid conditions of parts of north China, finds frequent and eloquent expression.

Myths of cultural benefits resemble those of other mythologies in two respects: deities are the divine originators of these benefits, and deities are the first to teach humans how to use them. Chinese culture deities are mostly masculine figures. Female deities often figure in cosmological myths, but their mythic narratives have been obscured for us by later scribal prejudice. Modern gender theory has rediscovered vestiges of their myths, such as the creator goddess and maker of humankind, and the mother goddesses of the sun and moon. Myths of dynastic foundation give a unique emphasis to female ancestors, followed by male founding figures, as with the Shang and Zhou origin myths. The theme of love is rare and is narrated in a sexually non-explicit manner, which may suggest early prudish editing. Divine birth is expressed through animalian agency, such as a bird or a bird's egg, or through parthenogenesis, for example from the belly of a male corpse, or an old woman's ear, or a hollow tree. Metamorphosis colours the stories, with objects turning into trees of brilliant and symbolic foliage, or figures becoming a bear, a bird or a star. The foundation motif becomes more frequent in later classical texts as dynastic rulers, ethnic peoples and major families claimed divine descent through populous and conflicting genealogical lines.

Themes of divine warfare and cosmic destruction are significant. There are also the important themes of a second beginning of the world after a hero has saved humankind from a major catastrophe, and of a Golden Age of wise kings who are ideal rulers and inaugurate the first human government. Less strong are themes to do with agriculture, the pastoral life, migration, exodus and exile, odyssey and the epic, and gender conflict. A major theme is the perception of foreigners in myths of the self and the cultural 'other'. Recurring themes of the warrior and the moral hero are represented in numerous episodes. Chinese heroic myth differs from other mythologies in its early emphasis on the moral virtue of the warrior hero.

Many figures depicted in mythical episodes represent cultural archetypes. The saviour figure occurs in myths that feature the creator goddess and the first human giant whose body becomes the universe. The archetype of the nurturing deity is represented by female cosmological and calendrical figures, such as the mothers of the sun and moon, and by the numerous male culture gods. Divine vengeance is symbolized by the myths of Woman Droughtghoul and Responding Dragon, who execute other deities on the command of a great god. There also appears the archetype of the failed hero, and the archetypal trickster figure, though these are not fully delineated in the myths. The stereotype of the successful hero figure is represented in several myths, for example the grain deity Sovereign Millet and the queller of the deluge, Reptilian-Pawprint. The moral hero Hibiscus is the archetypal hero and the leader of his people. These themes, archetypes, symbols and motifs will be developed and explored in the following chapters.

Origins

The creation of the world

China has a rich tradition of creation myth. There are six separate narratives in which different figures have a major role and function. One of the earliest creation myths centres on the archaic goddess named Woman Gua (Nu Gua). The name 'Gua' means a snail-like creature; insects and reptiles that cast off their shell or skin were believed to have the power of regeneration. Her myths are partly obscured by the gender bias of medieval commentators, yet they are present, although elusively in the earliest texts. It is related that Woman Gua made seventy transformations from which the cosmos and all living things took shape. Her divinity was so potent that her guts metamorphosed into ten deities called the Guts of Woman Gua.

Another creation myth is told by the Daoist author, the philosopher Zhuang Zi of the fourth century BC. He used ancient myth to illustrate several philosophical views, such as the danger of political intervention and mis-

The archaic goddess Woman Gua (Nu Gua).

The deity Muddle Thick (Hundun).

guided charity. The creation myth told in his book *Zhuang zi* concerns the myth of the dying god of chaos, whose destruction is necessary for the universe to take shape. It centres on Muddle Thick (Hundun), who had no face or facial apertures. The god Hundun ruled the centre of the world, with the gods of the southern and northern waters ruling on each side. These two sea gods visited Hundun often, and in return for his hospitality they decided that since he had no face they would give him seven openings so he could see, hear, eat and breathe. They chiselled an opening each day, but on the seventh day Hundun died. In another text this god of chaos is described as looking like a yellow sack and as red as cinnabar flame, with six feet and four wings, but without a face or eyes.

A third creation myth represents a vivid world picture. It relates that out of primeval vapour the two cosmic forces of Yin and Yang emerged. Through their interaction the cosmos took shape. The sky appeared as a round canopy that covered the four-sided flat earth, with the sky and the earth held together by massive mountains (or in a variant, pillars) fastened by cords. The world picture of this creation myth is so similar to ancient Egyptian cosmology that it may reflect a cultural transmission from Egypt through Central Asia.

A fourth myth gives more details about the cosmic forces of Yin and Yang. It relates that before the world began there was only a formless expanse of vapour. From this primeval element were produced the Yin force, which is dark, cold, shaded, heavy, feminine and passive, and the Yang force, which is light, hot, sunny, ethereal, masculine and active. The interaction between Yin and Yang created the four seasons and the natural world. Yang gave birth to fire and the sun; Yin gave birth to water and the moon, and then the stars.

The myth of the separation of the sky and the earth belongs to creation narratives. It tells of a monstrously deformed sky god called Fond Care (Zhuan Xu) who rules the pivot of the sky. He commanded his grandson

The giant Coiled Antiquity (Pan Gu).

Chong to prop up the sky for eternity, and his other grandson Li to press the earth down forever. It was believed in antiquity that if the two elements of sky and earth were not kept separate, the cosmos would return to chaos.

The most colourful creation myth centres on the giant Coiled Antiquity (Pan Gu), the first-born, semi-divine human being. It tells how he lay dying and as his life ebbed away his breath became the winds and clouds, his voice thunder, his eyes the sun and moon, and his limbs mountains. His bodily fluids turned into rain and rivers, his flesh into the soil. His head hair became the stars, his body hair became vegetation. His teeth, bones and marrow turned into minerals. The insects on his body became human beings. This myth is made up of a series of metamorphoses in which the various parts of the body became analogous parts of the universe. It is one of many myths of the cosmological human body from around the world, and it contains the important myths of the dying god and the nurturing god, who gave his body for the benefit of humankind.

Another version of the Coiled Antiquity myth relates that at the beginning of time all matter was like a chicken's egg. After eighteen thousand years it separated into the Yang ethereal matter that rose to form the sky and the

The Three Sovereign Deities.

Yin heavy matter that sank to form the earth. Coiled Antiquity was born between these sacred primordial elements as they unfolded. The giant went through nine metamorphoses and became as divine and wise as the sky and earth. Eighteen thousand years later the sky, the earth and the first human reached their maximum size and formed a trinity of Heaven, Earth and Humankind. Later on, Three Sovereign Deities emerged (their names vary). The narrative goes on to tell how numbers were created and cosmic distances were fixed, and it provides the etiological myth of the science of mathematics.

The two creation myths of Coiled Antiquity are the latest in textual terms among the six narratives, and they derive from a minority ethnic group of south-western China. Recorded in around the third century AD, they were probably transmitted from Central Asia. Of the two, the first, the myth of the cosmological human body, became the orthodox account of the creation of the world in China.

The creation of humankind

Myths of the creation of human beings are told in three stories. The earliest story is found in the creation myths of Yin and Yang, who produced all living things out of primeval vapour, including crawling creatures and human beings. The story of the death of Coiled Antiquity relates that the insects on his body turned into the first humans. A third myth of the origin of humans is told in a dramatic and colourful way. It centres on the creator goddess Woman Gua and the story begins after the creation of the world. It tells how Woman Gua kneaded yellow clay like a potter and made images of humans which then came to life. She wanted to create more but could not, so she made a furrow in the mud with her builder's cord and lifted the cord in and out of the mud, the falling mud turning into human form. Woman Gua's divine emblems are a knotted cord and a compass.

The myth goes on to explain the origin of social hierarchy. The yellow clay humans became the ruling class of rich and noble people, while the mud produced the mass of the poor and servile underclass. The colour motif of yellow resonates through Chinese culture. The deity called the Great God Yellow (Huang Di) became the supreme god of philosophical and religious Daoism. Yellow also symbolizes the divine Earth, and the centre of the human world. It became the emblematic colour of some dynasties.

The origins of culture and human society

China has numerous myths of the origins of culture and human society. These are etiological myths which contain the statement that a certain deity 'was the first to' grant a gift of culture, or that a deity 'taught humans how to use' the divine gift. It is emphasized that it was the deities who invented and discovered cultural benefits rather than humans, and this conveys the idea of divine control over human life.

Most of the cultural benefits are granted by male deities. The myth of

The Farmer God (Shen Nong) with his forked plough. The inscription reads: 'The Farmer God taught agriculture based on land use; he opened up the land and planted millet to encourage the myriad people'.

the Farmer God (Shen Nong) relates how he taught humans the uses of medicine and the benefits of agriculture. The god took pity on humans who were suffering illnesses from eating toxic plants and drinking contaminated water. The Farmer God tasted all the plants and taught humans the difference between the poisonous and the edible. His method was to thrash plants with his rust-coloured whip and to judge their value by their taste and smell. He organized plants into four categories: the bland, the toxic, the cool and the hot. This taxonomy forms the basis of traditional Chinese medicine, and the deity became the divine patron of medicine. The Farmer God also showed humans how to distinguish between types of soil and land. He created a wooden plough and taught humans how to till the soil and sow the five grains: hemp, wheat (or barley), leguminous crops and two types of millet. His agricultural function overlaps with that of the grain deity Sovereign Millet (Hou Ji). The emblem of the Farmer God is a forked plough.

The culture myth of the grain deity features the important figure Sovereign Millet. The name of this deity may refer to a male or female figure. In other mythologies, the grain or cereal deity and the earth deity are usually represented as female figures because they symbolize fertility and birth. A long narrative poem from the Zhou *Classic of Poetry* relates how Sovereign Millet taught humans how to sow grain, cook it, and offer it in sacrifice as the first food of thanksgiving from humans. This deity also features in the myth of the origins of the early Chinese and the second historical dynasty, the Zhou.

A god who appears later in the mythological tradition is Fu Xi, whose name means Prostrate (Sacrificial) Victim. The myths of his invention of writing, divination and hunting weapons is told through the device of mimesis – that is, the imitation of an observed act and its application to an analogous method. The narrative relates that at the time when Prostrate Victim ruled the cosmos he looked at the sky and the earth and observed the markings of birds and beasts, and he contemplated their images and patterns. With this knowledge, which was based on the natural order of things, the god created the first written symbols of the Eight Trigrams for humans to make divination. Eight Trigrams (*Ba Gua*) originally referred to a set of eight combinations of three broken and unbroken lines (broken denotes Yin female, unbroken denotes Yang male); these eight were multiplied to make a set of sixty-four, and the three lines were doubled to make six; the sixty-four variations of six lines formed the basis of a system of divination; they were given titles, and explanations were attached to them, which were recorded in the *Classic of Change* (Yi jing). Prostrate Victim also watched a spider weaving its web, and he fashioned knotted cords into nets and taught humans how to use them for hunting and fishing. This god is represented in art with his emblem of a carpenter's square; he has a human form with a snake's tail. In the late classical era, around the first century BC, he was linked to the primeval creator goddess Woman Gua as the first divine married couple, with their tails intertwined to symbolize mating.

The mythical figure of Chi You, whose name translates as Jest Much, has the function of the war god and the inventor of metal weapons. His myth presents the etiology of metal, the art of metallurgy and the invention of weapons. It relates that two mountains burst open and poured out water and metal. The god gathered the metal and made weapons and armour from it. He formed a powerful group with his seventy-two brothers, who all had bronze heads and ate stone pebbles. Jest Much is represented as an ox with horns and hooves. Through his discovery of metallurgy he achieved supremacy among the gods.

Woman Gua (left) holding her compass and Prostrate Victim (Fu Xi) holding his carpenter's square. Their tails are intertwined to symbolize mating.

左右三

The Qin emperor attempts to retrieve a sacred cauldron that flew into the Si River.

The myth of the origin of metal and metal-working is told also through the important figure of the semi-divine hero Yu, whose name means Reptilian-Pawprint. It tells how Reptilian-Pawprint forged nine sacred bronze cauldrons which were engraved with the knowledge of the world. He showed humans how to distinguish between monsters and benign beings in their passage through life. These bronze cauldrons were endowed with the sacred power of judging moral worth and were handed down from dynasty to dynasty. If the ruler was virtuous and governed the people kindly, the cauldrons were heavy with moral power and remained with the ruler and his dynasty. If the ruler was evil and mistreated the people, the cauldrons became light and flew away. These sacred vessels served as a symbol of legitimate dynastic rule and as emblems of wealth, ritual and state control over the strategic production of metal weapons and goods.

The origin myth of sericulture, the preparation of silk, is a distinctively Chinese story. It is told that the god Silkworm Cluster (Can Cong) was a divine silkworm who produced prolific amounts of silk. He ruled the people of Shu in the south-west (modern Sichuan province). He taught his people about silkworms and the mulberry tree leaves which were their food. Silkworm Cluster made several thousand golden silkworms and gave one each to his people. These multiplied and produced huge cocoons, and the people were able to return the gift of their produce to the god-king. On his divine progress around Shu, people would gather at his stopping places, and these became the first markets.

The discovery of harmony and musical instruments is related in numerous myths, and different deities are said to have granted these gifts to humans. Among them are Prostrate Victim (Fu Xi), who created music patterned on the divine harmony of the cosmos and handed it down to humankind, and the Great God Tellswift (Ku), who commanded two deities, one of whom was You Chui (or Skill Weights), to compose tunes and make drums, bells and pipes for humans to play. The most extended narrative of the myth of the origin of music centres on the son of the hero Yu whose name was Open, Lord of the Summer. Open is described as wearing green snakes through his ears and riding a pair of dragons. He was carried into the sky and there he received the gift of the music of Heaven. The titles of this music are reflected in the second early poetry anthology of China, *Songs of Chu*, such as the hymns to river goddesses entitled 'The Nine Songs', dating from around the fourth century BC. The *Songs of Chu* belongs to the ancient culture of the Huai and Yangtze River region in south China.

The ancient text, the *Classic of Mountains and Seas*, is a treasure trove of classical myth, and it features episodes of more than two hundred mythical figures. Among them are numerous culture deities, such as Turncorner (Fan Yu) who invented boats, Lucky Glare (Ji Guang) who invented wooden carts, Turnabout (Ban) who made bows and arrows, Reap Even (Shu Jun) who made the first ox-drawn plough, and Skill Weights (You Chui or Qiao Chui), who was the first god to come down to earth and bring humans all the arts of skilled craftmanship.

It is a characteristic of myth that some figures are so potent they inspire cycles of myth stories in which their earliest recorded roles may change and even become diminished. This is evident in the myth of the first marriage in human society. The story tells how Woman Gua and her unnamed brother wanted to make love but were ashamed, so they decided to ask god for permission. God performed a miracle to show his approval, and so the first humans made love. But they hid their shamed faces behind a grass fan. This rare account of an incestuous marriage may contain a rationale for breaking the taboo against marriage between close relatives in times of dire need, such as floods, famine, war or epidemics which destroy populations and threaten the survival of the human race. This myth may be compared with that of the divine marriage of Woman Gua the creator goddess to the god Prostrate Victim. The myth of Woman Gua's marriage to her brother was first recorded in the medieval period, by Li Rong (fl. AD 846–74), when attitudes to women were prejudiced and the position of women was devalued. It reveals how the potent goddess, who created the world and humankind and was the saviour of the world in the catastrophe of fire and flood, became demoted during the period between the classical and medieval eras from a divinity to a human being.

The myth of the first government

The myth of the first human government is narrated by an anonymous classical writer in the *Classic of History* (also known as *Ancient History*). The mythic story he tells illustrates the way a writer uses old myths and interprets them to create a completely new myth, a process called mythopoeia. The author starts his story at the beginning of time: not in the age of the deities, but when the first ideal rulers named Yao and Shun governed the world. When Yao became very old he wanted to abdicate, but he refused to bequeath the throne to his son. Instead, he passed it on to his worthy minister Hibiscus (Shun), to whom he also gave his two daughters in marriage. Shun then formed the first government. He made the hero Reptilian-Pawprint (Yu) the Superintendent of Flood Control Works, and Kui the Director of Music. He made Breath and Blend (Xi and He), two male officials, responsible for regulating the agricultural calendar in the Board of Astronomy. He made Sovereign Millet the Minister of Agriculture. It has already been seen that Sovereign Millet was the primeval grain deity. Similarly, we will see (in later chapters) that Reptilian-Pawprint was a semidivine hero who brought the world flood under control, and that Kui was a one-legged thunder god. Also, Breath Blend was one deity, the omnipotent sun goddess who was the mother of the ten suns. It is clear that the anonymous writer of the *Classic of History* used familiar figures in the old myth narratives to invent a new story which would tell how the first human government came to be formed. In his story, the ideal rulers Yao and Shun are succeeded by the virtuous Yu to become a triumvirate in the Golden Age of Antiquity, when government was founded on moral values.

Origin myths of the first historical dynasties

Fragments of myth in the Zhou *Classic of Poetry* relate the myths of the divine origins of the Shang and the Zhou dynasties. The Shang origin myth tells how the sky god commanded a divine dark bird to come down from Heaven to earth and give birth to the Shang. Another version appears in the much later first history of China, written by Sima Qian *c.* 100 BC, *Records of the Grand Historian (Shi ji)*. He narrates that a lovely girl called Bamboo-slip Maid (Jian Di) went to bathe. She saw a black bird drop its egg and picked it up and swallowed it. She became pregnant and gave birth to a boy named Xie (pronounced Shieh, also known as Qi, pronounced Chee). Jian Di became the divine ancestress of the Shang people, and her son by virgin or miraculous birth became the male founder of the Shang dynasty.

The myth of the divine origin of the Zhou is told in the same texts. This relates that the girl Jiang Yuan (Jiang the Originator) trod in the big toeprint of a great god and became pregnant. She gave birth to a child called Sovereign Millet. But Jiang Yuan thought her child was unlucky, so she tried to abandon it. She left it in a narrow lane where cattle went, but the cattle suckled the child and protected it. She then left it in some woods, but people from the plains who went to cut wood found the child and rescued it. She then laid her child on ice, but birds raised it on their feathers and kept it warm. Her divinely born child was destined to achieve great things, and despite enduring these three trials the child hero survived. Then Jiang Yuan nurtured her baby, who grew up to possess a divine knowledge of seed culture, especially of millet, and also the vegetal culture of beans. The young hero taught humans these arts. This divinely born person became the grain deity who also taught humans how to cook millet and offer it in sacrifice to Sovereign Millet, the grain deity and the founder of the Zhou people and the Zhou dynasty.

Divine cosmos

Several hundred mythical figures and deities crowd the pages of classical texts. One text alone, the *Classic of Mountains and Seas*, features 204 individual deities and mythical figures, with a total of 237 if several groups of divinities are included. The texts divide into two broad categories: those which present a large number of figures, male and female, with diverse functions and significance, and those which project a distinctively masculine pantheon with a limited number of divine functions. The former, more comprehensive category of texts contains material which belongs to a mythological tradition that has parallels with myths from other cultures. The second category of texts includes those which use mythical figures in a new, inventive way, such as the *Classic of History*, and this category of texts broadly speaking formed the orthodox canon in China. Modern studies of Chinese myth now explore those other texts which fall outside the textual boundary of orthodoxy and are rediscovering much that has previously been overlooked or neglected in Chinese mythology.

The pantheon of the deities and their functions

There is no fixed pantheon in Chinese mythology. The category of orthodox texts which focus on masculine figures generally mentions a limited sequence of about ten major deities and mythical figures which forms a loosely structured pantheon. The following sequence is typical: Prostrate Victim (Fu Xi), the Farmer God, the fire god Flame (Yan Di), the Great God Yellow (Huang Di), the god of light Young Brightsky (Shao Hao), the sky god Fond Care (Zhuan Xu), the Great God Tellswift (Ku), and the semi-divine ideal rulers Lofty, Hibiscus and Reptilian-Pawprint (Yao, Shun and Yu).

In contrast, the more comprehensively mythological texts are teeming with deities. The supreme gods mentioned in the *Classic of Mountains and Seas* are the god Foremost (Jun), and then Fond Care, but the major deity of the masculine tradition, Prostrate Victim, does not even appear in that book. Its other major deities include Queen Mother of the West, the sun-mother

Breath Blend (Xi He) and the moon-mother Ever Breath (Chang Xi), and it is true to say that this text gives greater emphasis to the feminine.

The divine functions of male deities relate to cultural benefits, such as agriculture through the Farmer God, Sovereign Millet and Sovereign Earth (Hou Tu), fire through the great god Flame, writing and divination through Prostrate Victim, the hunt through Yi the Archer and war through Jest Much, besides the benefits of weaponry, musical instruments, transport and craftsmanship which are all gifts of male gods.

The divine functions of female deities involve cosmogony, calendrical systems, nurturing roles, paradisial bliss and sacred violence. The goddess Breath Blend (Xi He) gave birth to the ten suns of the archaic calendrical week and nurtured them. The goddess Ever Breath (Chang Xi) gave birth to the twelve moons and nurtured them. Woman Gua created the cosmos (in one version of the creation myth), rescued the world from the catastrophes of fire and flood in her role as the divine smith and the saviour of humankind, and she created humankind. The Queen Mother of the West (Xi Wang Mu) has two functions: she sends plagues and punishments down to earth, but she also presides over the western mountain paradise.

Male and female deities are theroanthropic, that is, having animalian features, such as serpentine tails, tiger fangs, bovine horns and avian wings, which are emblems respectively of fertility, ferocity, aggression and aerial flight. Queen Mother of the West is represented with wild hair, the fangs of a tigress, and a panther's tail. Three bluebirds bring her food. In the later tradition she is accompanied by a nine-tailed fox and guarded by a leopard. Many deities are represented with snakes in their ears and riding dragons through the sky. The deities and mythical figures in the orthodox, masculine tradition, especially in classical Confucian texts, are represented as humanized beings who bear functional emblems, such as the human figure of the Farmer God with his plough and Reptilian-Pawprint the flood-queller with his dredger.

The names of many deities indicate their rank in a divine hierarchy and also show their function and gender. The term *Di* (pronounced Dee) is generally attached to male deities, such as Huang Di or Di Ku, and has the meaning of 'great god', giving the Great God Yellow and the Great God Ku (translated as Tellswift). Frequently the term *Di* appears without a name: this does not refer to a God Almighty, but to some unknown great god. The names of great goddesses often include 'stopgap' titles such as *Nu* (Woman), *Huang* (Grace), and *E* (Sublime), as with Nu Gua and Sublime Grace (E Huang). Otherwise they are known by their function, such as Breath Blend, the sun goddess, and Woman Droughtghoul (Nu Ba), the female bringer of drought. Lesser divinities are known as *Shen* (Divine or Holy Being, or god). *Ling* means divine power. *Gui* refers to a ghostly divinity. *Shi* with a name is used for a corpse deity, such as the Corpse of Prince Night and the Corpse of the Yellow Giantess. Then there are motley demons, imps and bogies that live in the mountains and streams or guard the gates of Heaven.

Miraculous birth

There are many differences between the gods and goddesses of other mythologies and those of Chinese myths, but none is so striking as the treatment of divine sexuality and procreation. Chinese myths do not include episodes of savage lust inspired by demonic energy. Instead they either refer to sex in a minor way or relate no sexual episodes at all. For example, the Great God Tellswift was the consort of two major goddesses who bore divine sons, but Tellswift was not their father. One of his goddess wives was Bamboo-slip Maid (Jian Di), who (as we have seen) swallowed the divine egg of the dark bird and was miraculously fertilized, giving birth to the male founder of the Shang dynasty. The other wife of Tellswift was Jiang Yuan who (as already mentioned) stepped in the big toeprint of a great god and was miraculously impregnated, giving birth to the founder of the Zhou dynasty. The myth of the divine birth of Reptilian-Pawprint (Yu), the flood hero, relates that he was born from the belly of the corpse of his father Gun, who had been executed by God. The story of the birth of Reptilian-Pawprint's own son is equally miraculous. Yu mated with the daughter of a mountain people, but one day he revealed himself in his divine aspect of a bear. His pregnant wife fled in terror and turned into a stone. Yu followed her and commanded the stone mother to give forth his son. The stone split open and Yu's son Open was born.

The children of virgin birth are usually male. It is possible that by the time the archaic oral tradition of myths was set down in writing they were often told in the idiom of a patriarchal culture. The myth of the Country of Women is the only one that narrates the survival of female infants; the males are left to die before they reach their third year. In this myth the fertilization of virginal women comes from bathing in a miraculous yellow pool.

Many myths of miraculous birth narrate stories of a virgin birth through the egg of a divine bird. This has been seen in the myth of the origin of the Shang people and their dynasty. Besides this form of ornithomorphous hierogamy, birth also occurs through other similar means. The semi-divine founder of a southern ethnic people, the Yao, was born as a worm in the ear of an old palace lady. The worm grew into a dog and became a hero in a time of war.

Although many myths relate narratives of virgin birth from divine goddesses or semi-divine female figures, in the later tradition it is the male gods who give birth through parthenogenesis, without female agency. Many such myths are genealogical foundation myths that relate the lineage of a country, a people or a notable family.

Divine warfare

The wars of the deities are narrated in several myths. There is the struggle for power between the god of war, Jest Much (Chi You), and the Great God Yellow. When the god of war discovered metal and invented metal weapons he threatened the supremacy of other deities. The Great God Yellow fought

The god of war, Jest Much (Chi You), inventor of metal weapons.

The god of war is executed by Responding Dragon (Ying Long).

with the god of war and defeated him through his two allies, his daughter the drought goddess named Woman Droughtghoul (Nu Ba) who dried up the war god's weapon of rain, and Responding Dragon (Ying Long) who killed him at Cruelplough Earthmound. Another myth relates that the rebellious worker god Common Work (Gong Gong) challenged the sky god Fond Care (Zhuan Xu) for divine supremacy. In his fury Common Work butted against one of the world mountains called Not Round that propped up the sky. This caused a flaw in the cosmos, so that the sky, sun, moon and stars tilted towards the north-west and the rivers and silt on earth flowed in a south-eastern direction. This narrative forms the etiological myth of the tilt of the earth.

A tragic conflict is told in one of the myths of Hugefish (Gun). He tries to save the world from the deluge by stealing god's divine cosmos-repairing soil called breathing-earth. But before he can use it, god commands his executioner, the fire god Pray Steam (Zhu Rong), to kill Hugefish on Feather Mountain. Hugefish's body does not decompose, however, and his son, the hero Reptilian-Pawprint (Yu), is born from his belly. Then Hugefish metamorphoses into a yellow bear (in variants, a turtle or dragon).

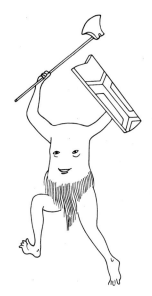

Another divine figure, named Boast Father (Kua Fu), is executed for an act of hubris. He challenged the divine power of the sun to race with him to the place where the sun sets. But Boast Father became parched with thirst, and even though he drank from a great river it was not enough. Before he could reach the next river he died of thirst, and his abandoned stick turned into a grove of trees. In another myth of a doomed hero, the warrior god named Heaven Punished (Xing Tian) challenges god for supremacy. God decapitates him and buries his head on a mountain, but the warrior god uses his nipples to make eyes and his navel for a mouth, brandishing his shield and battleaxe in a war dance.

Heaven Punished (Xing Tian).

Death of the gods

The myth of the dying god is expressed through several figures. Muddle Thick (Hundun), the god of chaos, has to die in order for the cosmos to be created. Hugefish must die because he committed the crime of theft from god. Boast Father is killed for his hubris. Jest Much is executed after his defeat by the Great God Yellow in a titanic struggle. Although it is related that the gods and goddesses die, they continue to live in another form through metamorphosis. Woman Lovely (Nu Wa) drowned in the East Sea, perhaps because she was trespassing or because, as the daughter of the Great God Flame, her own divine power became extinguished. She was transformed into a bird and renamed Sprite Guard (Jing Wei), and for the rest of eternity she tries to dam up the East Sea in revenge.

The myth of the fearsome god called Notch Flaw (Ya Yu) relates a rare rite of resuscitation by shamans. Notch Flaw was killed by two warriors, Twain Load (Er Fu) and Peril (Wei). Six shamans nurtured his corpse and held the drug of immortality over it. The myth does not say whether Notch Flaw was revived and turned into another shape, but it does go on to tell how his murderers were executed by god for their crime. God had them manacled with their own hair and strung up on a tree on the top of a mountain, and left them exposed for birds and beasts to eat. Two other gods who killed another deity were also executed, and they turned into ominous birds of prey which foretold the coming of a great war and drought.

Divine paradise

Several myths relate how deities descend to earth and create paradises in which to enjoy the human world. These paradises have names like God's Bedroom or God's Secret City on Earth. The most famous of these is the four-sided plateau on Kunlun Mountain. This mighty range stretches from north-west China across northern Tibet and ends in northern Afghanistan. It is the most vivid representation of the mythic motif of the celestial archetype. This western mountain paradise, guarded by the ferocious Openbright (Kai-ming) animal, has wells that are always full of fresh water, a precious jewel tree, and fabulous flora and fauna. The goddess Queen Mother of the West reigns on one of its peaks.

Another paradise myth tells of five mountain islands in the eastern sea where deities and immortals live. One day these Isles of the Blest start to drift towards the western ends of the world and are close to destruction. So god commands the giant god of the northern sea, Ape Strong (Yu Jiang), to secure the islands by making fifteen gigantic turtles hold the island paradises on their heads, taking it in turns to bear the load.

Catastrophe myths

Classical writers were keenly aware of the catastrophes which affected human society. It is recorded in a book of the third century BC that the statesman and philosopher Guan Zi, who lived in the seventh century BC, made this assessment of perennial disasters: 'Floods are one, droughts another, wind, fog, hail and frost are another; pestilence is one and insects another . . . Of the five types of disaster, floods are the most serious.' This chapter deals with myths of flood, drought and fire.

The flood myth

The most enduring and widespread of the catastrophe myths worldwide is the flood myth. In classical China the myth is told in four stories. The myth of the rebellious worker-god Common Work (Gong Gong) relates how he stirred the waters of the whole world so that they crashed against the barrier of the sky and threatened the world with chaos. This flood myth is the only one which gives the cause of the flood and the figure who started it. In this version the god Common Work plays the role of the marplot, one who seeks to destroy the design of the cosmos. In this respect, it is linked to the myth which tells how Common Work challenged the supreme sky god, Fond Care (Zhuan Xu), and in his fury butted against the world mountain that held up the sky.

Another flood story tells how the goddess Woman Gua saved the world from raging fires and a deluge. In her role as the divine smith, Woman Gua smelted the cosmic five-coloured stone and restored the sky. Then she cut the legs off a giant turtle and propped up the four corners of the earth and sky. She also dammed the flooding waters with the ashes of burnt reeds.

A third story features the heroic Hugefish (Gun), who is described in one text as the first-born son of god. Unfortunately, this flood myth is narrated in a passage that is garbled. The text itself, 'Questions of Heaven' of the fourth century BC, is presented as a series of questions or riddles about the early myths and legends of China. Piecing the story together, the following account emerges. A group of lesser gods urge god to choose Hugefish to deal with the crisis afflicting the world when there is a great deluge. Although god commands Hugefish to control the flood waters, he is uneasy about this choice of hero. Two divine creatures, the owl (which knows the mystery of the sky) and the turtle (which knows the secrets of the waters), come to the hero's aid. But Hugefish can control the flood only by stealing god's miraculous breathing-earth, the cosmic soil which can repair the world. For this sacrilege of theft, god condemns Hugefish to death before he can use the magic soil. Hugefish is executed on Feather Mountain by the fire god Pray Steam, and left to rot from exposure. But his body does not decompose, and his son Yu is born from his belly. Then Hugefish is revived by shamans, and he turns into a yellow bear. In this myth Hugefish plays several roles: saviour, heroic victim, failed hero and dying god. His mythic function is to try to mediate between god and humankind to ensure the continuation of the world and the human race.

The fourth flood story proved to be the most potent and became the orthodox version of the classical Chinese flood myth. One narrative appears in the same passage of 'Questions of Heaven' which gives the flood myth of Hugefish. It is told that Reptilian-Pawprint (Yu) was favoured by god and was permitted to use the breathing-earth to repair the cosmos and control the flood. Another narrative appears in the philosophical writings of Mencius of the fourth century BC, who was an eloquent spokesman for the moral concepts of the Confucian school. As with other Confucian texts, the narrative of the Yu flood myth as told in *Mencius* is set in the mythical or pseudo-historical era of the beginning of human time, when Lofty (Yao) and Hibiscus (Shun) ruled the world. The story tells how a vast deluge threatened the world when the waters of all the rivers flowed out of their channels and flooded the Middle Kingdom (China). Snakes and dragons overran the land and the people had nowhere to live, so they made shelters in nests on the low

Reptilian-Pawprint (Yu) with his dredger. The inscription reads: 'Yu of the Hsia was skilled in charting the earth; he explored water sources and he understood the Yin [cosmic principle]; according to the seasons he constructed high dikes; then he retired and created the physical punishments.'

ground and lived in caves on the high ground. The ruler Hibiscus ordered Reptilian-Pawprint to control the flood water. Reptilian-Pawprint dug channels to conduct the water out to sea, and he drove out the snakes and dragons and expelled the rapacious birds and beasts. Humans were then able to return to their homes in the plains and resettle there. This narrative contains a number of important mythic motifs. The flood introduces the theme of a return to primeval chaos. The myth of the hero is exemplified by Reptilian-Pawprint's great labours as he struggles to restore order. There are also the themes of a second beginning of the world, of human survival, and the restoration of human society to its dominant position over the animal kingdom. The most significant motif is that the flood is finally ended not by divine intervention but through the agency of the moral hero, who puts his sense of public duty before private concerns and who performs his tasks with courage, obedience and virtue.

The myth of the world catastrophe by fire

The primary myth of a world conflagration features the hunter god, Yi the Archer. The Chinese graph or character for the name Yi shows joined hands and a pair of feathers. This myth provides a cause for the fiery inferno that threatens to extinguish the world. The solar myth of the sun goddess relates that she gave birth to ten suns, which she allowed to rise in turn each day. The myth tells how one day all ten suns rose together and threatened to parch the crops and scorch human beings. The hunter god Yi the Archer felt pity for humankind and asked a sky god, the Great God Foremost (Jun), if he would lend his divine aid to the world. The god gave Yi the Archer a divine vermilion bow and plain arrows with silk cords. The hunter god aimed at the suns and shot them down.

Another mythic narrative relates that nine searingly hot suns fell to earth and landed on a rock that was later named Whirlpool Furnace (Wu Jiao). This name combines the infinite power of the sea which extinguished the suns and the fiery furnace created by their molten remains. Yi the Archer features in several episodes and is linked to one of the moon goddesses and myths of monsters. These stories form a cycle of Yi the Archer myths.

Drought myths

The disaster of drought is told through several different myths. One relates that a drought lasted for five (in a variant, seven) years in the reign of one of the mythical founders of the Shang dynasty, the king named Tang the Conqueror. The king's people were reduced to starvation and thirst, and the royal diviners wanted to offer up human sacrifice to placate the gods and ancestral spirits. But the king chose a more selfless, heroic way to relieve the drought. He went to the sacred grove of Mulberry Forest and prayed to god to forgive human error by accepting himself as a sacrificial victim and removing the punishment of the drought. He said, 'If I, the One Man, have sinned, do not punish the people. If the people have sinned, let me alone take the

The hunter god Yi the Archer shoots down the suns, symbolized by birds in the world tree.

blame.' The king then prepared himself as if he were a sacrificial animal. He cut off his hair and fingernails, rubbed his hands smooth, and sprinkled water on himself. Then he was tightly bound with white rushes and driven to an open-air altar by white horses. (White was the emblematic colour of death.) He was placed on the woodpile, and just as the fire took hold a great downpour of rain fell. In this drought myth, unlike the flood myth stories, the reason for the disaster is given, that is, divine retribution for human error, and in this motif the myth parallels Biblical catastrophe myth and other myths worldwide. The drought myth reflects the semi-arid, drought-prone environment of the northern region of Shang culture, but it is not recorded in Shang writings.

Another drought story exists in fragmentary form. It features a corpse deity named Woman Deuce (Nu Chou). In this myth she plays the role of the victim, but the narrative does not say whether she chose this role or was compelled to do so. It tells how Woman Deuce was born a corpse goddess. At the time when the ten suns all rose at once, she stayed high up on a mountain to expiate human error. She tried to screen her face with her green sleeve or to hide her deformed, scorched face. But she was burned to death on the mountain by the merciless heat of the suns and she died again, to be reborn a goddess. Her green clothes are an emblem of vegetal renewal and the revitalizing power of rain. In another fragment it is related that the goddess Woman Deuce lived in the sea, and she is represented holding her emblematic crab. According to ancient belief the crab waxes and wanes with the moon and is also a creature that knows the sources of life-giving water.

Another narrative tells how the daughter of the Great God Yellow had the power of sending down drought to the human world. Her name was Woman Droughtghoul (Nu Ba). In the cosmic battle between the two gods, Yellow and the war god Jest Much, the war god chose rain as one of his weapons in the form of the rain god. But the Great God Yellow sent his daughter Woman Droughtghoul to dry up the source of rain and also sent his avenging ally Responding Dragon (Ying Long) to execute the god of war. This divine creature had the power to withhold rain or to make rain fall. A narrative also relates that after this war of the gods Woman Droughtghoul's divine power was diminished and she could not rise back into the sky. She remained on earth and caused havoc by drying up water ditches and irrigation channels. The people therefore learned to perform a rite to exorcise the baneful goddess, calling out: 'Goddess, go north!' This would send the goddess back to her place of exile.

Mythic heroes and heroines

The mythical figure of the hero appears in the different roles of the saviour, culture bearer, warrior and founder of a new race, tribe or dynasty. Of over twenty stereotypical features of the hero worldwide, the most frequent and widely distributed among myths of the hero are miraculous birth, the three trials or tests, the labours in performing the tasks, and divine aid from the natural or supernatural world. By hero both male and female figures are intended. Heroism is also characterized by acts of military courage, idealism, devotion to a cause, nobility of spirit, hubris, revenge and patriotism. These include both positive and negative traits, but a unique feature of the archetypal Chinese hero is his moral valour.

Three mythical figures exemplify the stereotypical features of the hero in Chinese mythology. They are Sovereign Millet, Hibiscus and Reptilian-Pawprint.

Sovereign Millet (Hou Ji)

Heroic features are clearly evident in myths of the grain deity Hou Ji, or Sovereign Millet. The earliest and most colourful myth of this figure appears in China's earliest poetry anthology, the *Classic of Poetry*. A long narrative poem tells how this deity was conceived after the goddess Jiang Yuan 'trod in the big toe of God's footprint'. After the birth of her child, Jiang Yuan wanted to get rid of it because she thought it was unlucky. The narrative relates the three trials of the child hero. First, as we have seen, she exposed it in a narrow country lane used by cattle, but the animals suckled the infant. Then the mother left her baby in a wood to die of exposure or to be eaten by wild animals. But woodcutters from the plains found and rescued it. Finally, she put her infant on freezing ice to die of cold, but birds warmed the child with their soft feathers and protected it with their large wings. The baby wailed so lustily that it was found, and its mother decided in the end to raise and nurture it. The child grew up to possess divine knowledge of cultivating beans and millet, and taught humans these arts. Sovereign Millet also taught people how to cook these crops and offer them in sacrifice in an act of

Jiang Yuan leaves her son Sovereign Millet (Hou Ji), the grain god, to die of cold on freezing ice, in the third trial of the child hero.

thanksgiving. The child hero became the grain deity and the founder of this people, the Zhou, from whom the ancient kings took the name of the Zhou dynasty.

Hibiscus (Shun)

The mythical figure of Hibiscus (Shun) centres primarily on his qualities as a moral hero and leader of people. His heroism is especially expressed through his sense of filial piety. His myths relate stories of how his family tried to destroy him, but in each of his trials or tests he responds with acts of filial duty, so that in the end he converts his family's murderous hatred into virtuous conduct. In the first episode of the three trials of Hibiscus, his father, who is called the Blind Man (Gu Sou), and his half-brother Elephant (Xiang) plot to kill him. They order him to repair the family grain store. Hibiscus is obedient, but his two resourceful wives warn him that his father and half-brother plan to set fire to the grain store and burn him alive. His wives tell him to wear his bird-patterned coat. When he goes up into the granary the Blind Man and Elephant remove the ladder and set fire to the building, but Hibiscus has already turned into a bird and flown away.

The second episode relates that the evil pair order Hibiscus to dig a well. Shun is obedient, but his two wives warn him of the plot and tell him to wear his dragon-patterned coat. The Blind Man and Elephant keep watch and, when Hibiscus has dug deep down, they start to fill in the well with the soil to bury him alive. But Hibiscus has already turned into a dragon and disappeared through the watery underworld.

The third trial of the hero Hibiscus tells how the Blind Man plots to kill him by plying him with strong alcohol. His two wives tell him to bathe himself with a magic lotion (in a variant, dog's mess). Hibiscus rubs it all over his body, and obediently drinks all the liquor his father gives him. But however much he drinks, he does not become intoxicated and remains sober throughout his ordeal.

Meanwhile, thinking that Hibiscus will die of alcohol poisoning, his family are busy dividing up his possessions between themselves. His half-brother has taken up residence in the home of Hibiscus and is playing on his lute when Hibiscus walks in. Full of amazement and shame, his half-brother Elephant makes excuses and denies any involvement in the plots. The story of the trials of Hibiscus ends with the words, 'Hibiscus once again served under the Blind Man and he loved his younger brother Elephant, and looked after him devotedly.'

This myth has several motifs that parallel myths of other cultures. The symbolism of the name, the Blind Man, signifies not just physical blindness but, in this story, moral ignorance as well. The barely sketched figure of the Blind Man's second wife, the stepmother of Hibiscus, reveals familiar character traits – cruelty to a young man, preference for her own child, and greed for her stepson's property – which occur in many fairy tales.

One of the earliest books to record the myth of Hibiscus, the filial son, was the *Mencius* of the fourth century BC. The philosopher Mencius was a major exponent of the humanistic doctrines of the Confucian school, and it was he in particular who first emphasized the ethical principle of filial piety. Through his teachings and especially through his narrative of the ordeals of Hibiscus (Shun), Mencius was instrumental in elevating this principle to an ideal standard in Confucian moral philosophy. Besides being endowed with the virtue of filiality, Hibiscus is one of the great heroes of the Golden Age of Antiquity, in the ideal rule of first Lofty (Yao), then Hibiscus (Shun), and finally the hero Reptilian-Pawprint (Yu).

Reptilian-Pawprint (Yu)

The mythical figure of Reptilian-Pawprint (Yu) shows most of the stereotypical features of the hero. He is born miraculously from the belly of his father's corpse. He is favoured by god, who aids him with the divine cosmic soil and the help of divine creatures to control the world flood. The labours of this hero were so great that it is told that his body shrivelled down one side and 'no nails grew on his hands and no hair grew on his lower legs'. He is the model of the successful hero in his role as queller of the world deluge. He also displays leadership qualities in the divine world when he calls the first assembly of the gods. He demonstrates his warrior spirit when he slays the nine-headed monster, Aide Willow (Xiang Liu), who was polluting the soil with his drool so that crops were spoiled. Reptilian-Pawprint stands as the saviour figure for these two heroic feats of calming the deluge and ridding the land of pollution. He also performs the superhuman task of measuring the whole world (in a variant, he deputes another god to do this). Moreover, to help humans make their way through a hostile world, he forges (in a variant, was presented with) nine sacred metal cauldrons which bore images of the good and bad knowledge of the cosmos. This hero is also the third of the three ideal rulers of the Golden Age, following Lofty and Hibiscus. It is related that Reptilian-Pawprint founded the mythical dynasty of the Xia (Summer), which traditional historians until recently have believed to be the first historical dynasty of China, before the historically verifiable Shang and Zhou dynasties.

Although the myth of the trials of the hero is not so clearly told among the many stories about Reptilian-Pawprint, the motif of the labours of the hero is emphatically expressed. The narratives of his labours tell of his physical powers of endurance, his power of survival, and his supernatural strength in restoring the world to the natural order. They also tell of his traits of character, how obedient he was to the command to undertake his superhuman tasks, and with what patience, self-sacrifice and bravery he pursued his goal to the finish. Among the traits of character that he displays, there is the singularly Chinese mythic motif of moral grandeur and moral integrity in his dutiful and devoted performance of the seemingly impossible tasks that are set for him.

The failed hero

The motif of the failed hero complements the dynamic function of the successful hero figure. The two types of hero are well represented by Hugefish (Gun) and his son Reptilian-Pawprint. There are many other examples of the failed hero in Chinese myth, who may be a deity or a semi-divine being, who struggles in a fair contest for supremacy but loses to a more formidable rival. Sometimes failure is caused by an all too recognizable human flaw, such as trickery or hubris. Yet the failed hero is sympathetically treated in Chinese myths. Examples of this motif include the figures of Hugefish, Jest Much the war god, Boast Father who raced with the sun, and the goddess Woman Lovely, who turned into the divine bird Sprite Guard.

These are deities and semi-divine figures whom the communal memory stubbornly refused to vilify or delete from early mythic narratives and later legend and folktale.

The archetypal saviour figure

The archetypal saviour figure is most clearly seen in catastrophe myth. Examples of the saviour figure include the creator goddess Woman Gua, who used her regenerative powers and her skill as the divine smith to repair the cosmos after it was damaged by the world fire and the world flood, and who rescued humankind from these catastrophes. Another example is the hunter god Yi the Archer, who saved the world from incineration when the ten suns rose together. Hugefish and Reptilian-Pawprint are both saviour figures but, whereas Hugefish failed because of his sacrilege of theft from god, Reptilian-Pawprint succeeded. The mythical Shang king Tang the Conqueror was also a heroic saviour, who offered himself up as a human sacrifice to placate the god who had sent down the punishment of a severe drought to the human world. Hugefish is the saviour figure who makes the ultimate sacrifice by giving his own life in his attempt to save the world from the flood.

Other mythic themes represent the archetype of the saviour figure. For example, the theme of the deities who bring benefits to humankind contains the motif of the divine wish to save human beings from a harsh environment and ensure their survival. The myth of the Farmer God, in particular, illustrates this motif. It narrates how the god suffered the pain and torment of tasting noxious plants so that he could show humans which plants were harmful and which were beneficial. Calendrical myths also feature a saviour figure who seeks to relieve the human world of deprivation and hardship. The deity Torch Dragon (Zhu Long), for example, shines his divine light in the north-western region where, it was believed, the sunlight did not reach. This deity is portrayed as scarlet, with a snake's body and a human head. When he shuts his vertical eyes it grows dark, and when he opens them it grows bright over the 'nine darknesses'. Torch Dragon has such care for the well-being of humans that he neither eats, sleeps nor rests.

The hero as slayer of monsters

A narrative of the solar catastrophe myth tells how the hunter god Yi the Archer shot down the nine extra suns in the sky, and at the same time killed monsters that were ravaging the land and plaguing the people. He slew six monsters: the human-devouring monster with a dragon's head called Notch Flaw (Ya Yu), the rapacious monster called Chisel Tusk, the voracious monster called Nine Gullets and the destructive bird Giant Gale, as well as the Giant Boar and the massive serpent Gianthead Snake. Yi the Archer was successful in his tasks of saving mortals. He shot down some monsters, executed others, beheaded the serpent at the numinous lake of Gushcourt, and captured the boar in the sacred grove of Mulberry Forest. In one version of this myth it is god who permits Yi the Archer to perform these saving acts, in others it is the ideal ruler Lofty (Yao) who commands the hero to do these tasks, and Lofty is rewarded by being made sovereign ruler by popular choice.

The hero Reptilian-Pawprint has many mythical functions, and one of these is as the warrior who slays a monster. During his labours to control the world flood, he has to destroy a giant creature that was polluting the people's land so that they could not grow their crops. As we have seen, this monster was called Aide Willow (Xiang Liu). He was the officer of the rebel worker-god Common Work. Aide Willow had a snake's body, coloured green, and nine heads with human faces. Each of his nine heads fed from different parts of the countryside at the same time, and everything the monster

Aide Willow (Xiang Liu).

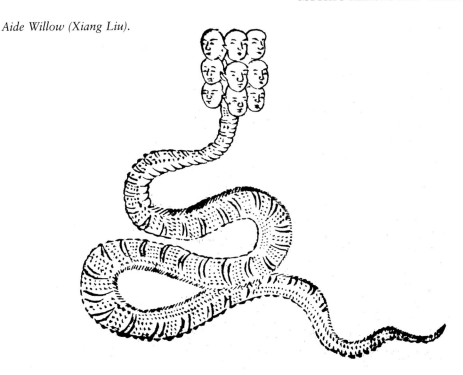

bumped into or his drool dripped on turned rancid and the soil was polluted. Reptilian-Pawprint slaughtered Aide Willow, but its blood flowed out copiously and it stank, polluting the earth even more. So the hero dug out the vile-smelling soil and let the monster's blood flow into these pits. But each time he dug, the pits overflowed with blood. In the end he used the soil that he had dug out to make a high terrace, where he worshipped the gods in thanksgiving for accomplishing his task of slaying the monster and subduing the flood.

The warrior hero

To the first historian of China, Sima Qian (*c.* 145–*c.* 186 BC), the mythical figure of the Great God Yellow (Huang Di) symbolized the fountainhead of Chinese culture and civilization. In the mythic narratives this deity is presented as a peace-loving culture bearer, and a warrior god who engages in purposeful battles with a series of enemies. His battles are not described in the rich detail of other mythologies, with their frenzy of fury and demonic anarchy. Of the Great God Yellow it is said in the narratives that he 'took no pleasure in war or aggression'. In one of the stories it is told how he fought with his brother, the Great God Flame. Each had ruled half the world with dual sovereignty, but then they contended for total supremacy. The two brothers fought with elemental weapons. Flame used the weapon of fire and Yellow used the weapon of water. The antithetical elements of fire and water led to the conquest of Flame by his brother Yellow.

The Great God Yellow (Huang Di). The inscription reads: 'The Yellow Emperor created and changed a great many things; he invented weapons and the wells and fields system; he devised upper and lower garments and established palaces and houses'.

It is also related that the Great God Yellow battled with the god of war and inventor of metal weapons, Jest Much. But again Yellow had the advantage, defeating the war god's weapon of rain with his daughter's weapon of drought. In this narrative the warrior god Yellow is said to have been challenged by the god of war, so that Yellow claimed divine right for his cause.

Another of Yellow's battles was with the thunder god Awestruck (Kui). Awestruck was a god in the form of an ox, with a blue body and only one leg. His radiance shone out like the sun and moon. But the Great God Yellow coveted Awestruck's power to make his thunderous sound heard throughout the cosmos, so he killed the thunder god and used his hide to make a drum. He killed another divine creature and used his bone as a drumstick, and then he beat on his cosmic drum so that 'the sound was heard for five hundred leagues and it made the world stand in awe'.

The fourth story of the battles of the warrior god Yellow relates that he was attacked by the Four Emperors, who were the gods of the four cardinal points. Great Whitelight was the green god of the east. Flame was the scarlet god of the south. Young Brightsky was the white god of the west. Fond Care was the black god of the north. Some of these gods have been mentioned before in narratives where they have different functions and roles. This story of Yellow's battle with the Four Emperors belongs to a somewhat later tradition, when the myths had begun to be altered. In earlier myth Fond Care (Zhuan Xu) is the great sky god, and Flame is the great god who was Yellow's brother and an omnipotent god. This later myth tells how the four gods plotted against Yellow and set up their military camp outside Yellow's city walls. But in the end Yellow defeated them.

It is clear that the early myths and some of the later myths of the Great

*The thunder god
Awestruck (Kui).*

God Yellow depict him first and foremost as a warrior god who is always successful against his enemies. Later Yellow became the supreme god of the philosophical school of Daoism and of the Daoist church. He also attracted a number of minor myths and folkloric tales which, taken together, form a cycle of myths of the Great God Yellow. Most importantly, this god became the ancestral deity of Chinese civilization through the sacred history of the people who were descended from the gods, ideal rulers and great heroes.

The motif of the warrior god also emerges in the mythic narratives of the semi-divine hero Reptilian-Pawprint. He is depicted in the role of a punitive deity who chastises the god Guard Gale (Fang Feng) for arriving late at the god's first assembly of the gods. Another story relates how Reptilian-Pawprint exiled the rebellious god Common Work when the former was given the task of controlling the flood. He also executed Common Work's officer, the nine-headed serpentine god called Aide Willow who had been polluting the farmers' crops.

Another strand of myth linked to the flood story tells how Reptilian-Pawprint had to subdue the turbulent river god of the Huai River of central China. This god looked like an ape, with an upturned snout and a high forehead. He had a green body, a white head and metallic eyes, and his neck was a hundred feet long. The river god was stronger than nine elephants together. So Reptilian-Pawprint asked his own ally Seven Dawn (Geng Chen) to help him capture the rebellious river god. In the end his neck was chained with a huge rope and a metal bell was threaded through his nostril, and he was banished to a distant mountain. After this, the water in the Huai River flowed peacefully out to sea.

Gender in myth

Modern works on the subject of gender have shown that neglected female figures can be rediscovered from accounts in traditional history and literature. Also, they reveal how the role of women can be brought to life from the silence of the ancient records. This new approach to the subject of the role of women in history and culture is particularly valuable for the rediscovery of previously unknown or undervalued female figures in Chinese mythology.

Some major examples include the figure of the great sun goddess Breath Blend (Xi He). Early myth narratives relate that she was the mother of the ten suns and that she nurtured them after their day's journey through the worldly sky. Some accounts say that she was the charioteer of the sun. But her role was gradually weakened and her functions transferred to masculine figures. The singular powerful goddess was made into two males, one called Breath (Xi) and the other called Blend (He), and they were said to be in charge of regulating the agricultural calendar.

In the same way the great primeval goddess Woman Gua, who had many roles and functions as creator and saviour, later became an inferior figure who was linked to the male god Fu Xi (Prostrate Victim), and was even turned into a human rather than a divine being.

When Chinese gender myths are examined closely they yield evidence of a significant number of important female roles. These include those of creator and saviour, cosmological and calendrical regulator, dynastic and genealogical founder, punitive and amorous roles, besides those of the trickster figure and the victim. The myths of Woman Gua show her functions as primeval creator, saviour in time of catastrophe, and inaugurator of the social institution of marriage. The sun goddess has the important functions of mother of the ten suns, purifier and fertilizer of the daily suns, and regulator of daylight and night-time and the yearly calendar with the proper rotation of her solar children. The primary moon goddess has similar functions in respect of her twelve lunar children. The other moon goddess, Ever Sublime (Chang E), is linked to the theme of immortality and rebirth as the spirit of the moon. She also plays the role of the trickster figure through her

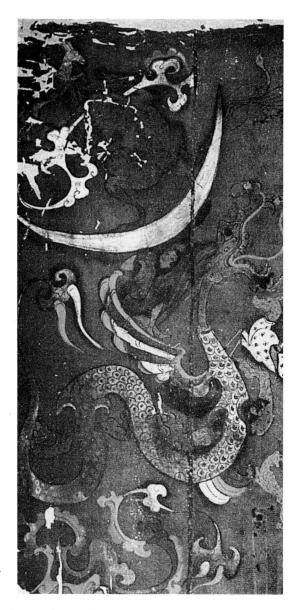

*The moon goddess Ever Sublime
(Chang E).*

theft of the drug of immortality from her consort, the hunter god Yi the Archer.

Two female divinities have the major function of dynastic ancestress. Bamboo-slip Maid (Jian Di) gave birth to the first of the Shang people, the male god who became the divine founder of the Shang dynasty. Jiang the Originator has a similar function as the mother of the first of the Zhou people, the deity called Sovereign Millet who founded the Zhou dynasty.

The *Classic of Mountains and Seas* is a valuable source of female myths, and among the classical texts of ancient China it constitutes one of the most sympathetic in its representation of the female mythical figure. In its last

47

The Queen Mother of the West seated on her leopard throne, attended by the nine-tailed fox and other figures.

chapters, especially, it relates the myths of numerous female ancestors who founded a genealogical line as a goddess, and who gave birth to deities who inaugurated a people or country. Among these little-known goddesses are Thunder Foremost (Lei Zu) and Hear Omen (Ting Yao).

Another major goddess is Queen Mother of the West. The earliest descriptions portray her as a wild and merciless goddess who punishes the human world with disease and disaster. She has a tangle of hair, the fangs of a savage tigress and a panther's tail. Her guardian animals are ferocious felines. But later writers softened her image, so that she became the goddess who granted immortality to humans and a civilized monarch who grants audience to historical Chinese emperors and conducts a graceful exchange of poems, songs and courtesies with human rulers.

Fragments of mythic narrative tell briefly of goddesses whose names suggest their function as avenging and punitive deities. They include Woman Killer (Nu Qian), Woman Destroyer (Nu Mie), Woman Battleaxe (Nu Qi) and Woman Sacrificer (Nu Ji).

The opposite role of woman as victim is seen in the myth of Woman Lovely (Nu Wa) who drowned and changed into a divine bird called Sprite Guard. The basic graph or character for 'Wa' means a frog. The same role is given to Woman Deuce, who was burned to death by the ten suns and became a corpse deity. As Woman Lovely the frog goddess died and changed into a bird, so too did a figure known as god's daughter, whose full myth is not known, turn into the tree which bears her name, the Silkmulberry-of-Godsdaughter.

The mythical role of divine lover is rare in Chinese mythology compared with other mythologies, especially those of Greece and Rome. But it is told in the stellar myth of Weaver Woman (Zhi Nu) and Oxherd, who were lovers separated by god as a punishment and allowed to meet in the sky just once a year, on the Seventh Night of the Seventh Moon, when Sky River (the Milky Way) could be forded.

Two features relating to gender are significant in Chinese mythology. One is the tendency for those deities which bestow gifts of culture, such as fire or medicine, on humankind to be male. The other is that females are not the only ones to give birth to offspring. Female births already mentioned are the sun-mother, the moon-mother, and the two divine ancestresses of the historical dynasties of the Shang and the Zhou, besides some genealogical goddesses. There is also the myth of virgin birth in the Country of Women, where women bathe in a fertilizing yellow pool and then produce children, allowing only the girls to survive. Many myths relate that birth is through a male parent, as with the birth of Reptilian-Pawprint through his father's belly. Numerous genealogical myths relate that male gods gave birth to other gods, who are usually male.

Weaver Woman (Zhi Nu) and Oxherd meeting in the sky.

Female mythical figures are sometimes designated by their names and titles. The clearest example is the 'stopgap' name 'Nu' meaning Woman. The terms Huang and E also denote females, such as Ever Sublime (Chang E) and Sublime Grace (E Huang). The gender of other goddesses is given in their name, such as 'Mu' meaning Mother in Queen Mother of the West. The gender of other figures is recognizable through the story of their myths, such as Bamboo-slip Maid (Jian Di) and Jiang the Originator.

In general, there are fewer female than male deities in the Chinese pantheon. Yet a significant number of female divinities are superior to, or equal to, male divinities in terms of role, function and cult in antiquity. It is in the evolution of the mythological tradition, with the changing social attitudes to male and female roles in the family and in public life, that the female role begins to be displaced by the male. This trend is seen in the latter part of the classical era when myths of female figures are minimally or obscurely narrated, and when the potency of female deities is diminished in various ways by male scribes who recorded and altered the myths. By the medieval period of around AD 1100, when classical texts were being codified and printed, the history of women was being rewritten by a male academic and literary hierarchy who shaped and altered the presentation of ancient myths according to new ideological belief-systems. This anti-female bias led to the disappearance of many significant female mythical figures from the mythological record. It is the task of students of modern Chinese myth to restore them to their true position and to re-evaluate their role in the mythological repertoire.

Metamorphoses

The dividing line between immortality and mortality in Chinese mythology is blurred, and the two states of being often merge. Although the primeval deities are by nature immortal, some die a death, whether by execution, mishap or other causes. Yet the transformational powers of divinities are so mysterious and their nebulous existence is so indefinable that even after death they live on, or parts of them live on in a changed state. Metamorphosis is the final destiny of mythical figures who are said to have been killed or have died.

Many are changed into plants, birds, animals or objects. When the god of war, Jest Much, was executed, his fetters turned into a grove of maple trees. When Boast Father died of thirst, his abandoned stick became Climbton Forest (Deng Lin). The mother of a hero and statesman named Officer Govern (Yi Yin) turned into a hollow mulberry trunk floating on a swollen river when she disobeyed an order in her dream not to look back at her flooded city.

Some mythical figures became metamorphosed into stars. Assistant Counsel (Fu Yueh) was the exemplary minister of the historical Shang dynasty king Wu Ding (c. 1200–1181 BC), and he was rewarded for his wisdom and humane administration by being immortalized as a star. There is also the myth of the two quarrelling brothers, Blocking Lord (Yan Bo) and Solid Sink (Shi Chen), who were punished by being turned into stars which were always apart and never met in the sky. The story of how the two stellar lovers Weaver Woman and Oxherd became stars is not known, but their unhappy love was such a popular theme that the story was told and retold in many versions.

Major myths relate how some figures turned into animals. When the divine hero Hugefish (Gun) failed in his task of quelling the flood and was executed for stealing god's magic soil, he turned into a yellow bear (in variants, turtle or dragon). His ursinity was passed on to his miraculously born son Reptilian-Pawprint, as we have seen. When his son had grown up and begun his task of controlling the flood, he met a girl from a mountain tribe and mated with her. One day he appeared to her by mistake in his bear shape. She fled from him and turned into a stone. He pursued her and commanded her to give him their son. The stone split open and his son was born. He was named Open.

The myth of one of the lunar goddesses, Ever Sublime (Chang E), tells how she turned into a toad when she stole her consort's drug of immortality and was wafted up to the moon. Other versions of her myth relate that the toad and the hare, symbols of regeneration and ingenuity, already lived on the moon, or that the hare (in a variant, the rabbit) was the goddess's pet.

Birds are the most frequent form of metamorphosis, perhaps because their winged flight images aerial divinity. The goddess Woman Lovely, who was the daughter of the great fire god Flame, turned into a bird named Sprite Guard after she drowned. Several fragmentary myths relate that the semi-divine ideal ruler Lofty (Yao) had a son named Cinnabar Crimson (Dan Zhu) of whom he disapproved. When Lofty decided to abdicate, he passed over his own son and gave the rulership of the world to his minister Hibiscus (Shun). The myth relates that Lofty exiled his son Cinnabar Crimson (in a variant, killed him), who turned into the bird of the hot fiery south named Crimsonowl (Zhu). This is a bird of omen that foretells the banishment of officials in the district where it appears. A similar destiny is recounted in the story of Mount Drum (Gu Shan) and Awe Osprey (Qin Pei). They were two mythical beings who murdered the god Lush River (Bao Jiang) and were hacked to death by a great god for this sacrilege. They metamorphosed into birds of prey. Awe Osprey became a giant osprey with black markings, a scarlet beak and tiger claws. It is an omen of war. Mount Drum became a bird like a kite, with scarlet feet and yellow markings. It is an omen of drought. Avian metamorphosis is also related in the myth of a king of the south-western region of Shu (modern Sichuan province). His tragic story tells how this ruler, named King Watch (Wang), heard of a man who had been found as a corpse floating in the river and who had come to life again. King Watch made him his minister. Later there was a flood in his kingdom and the king could not control it. So he sent this minister to the outlying region of his kingdom to deal with the flood water. While the minister was away, the king committed adultery with his wife. But afterwards he was so full of shame that he abdicated in favour of his minister and went into self-imposed exile. The king turned into a nightjar. When people hear the call of the nightjar they say it is the soul of King Watch.

The mythic motif of metamorphosis was used by the Daoist philosopher Zhuang Zi to explain difficult ideas of relative perspective, subjectivity and objective reality. In one of his vivid explanations of these themes he narrates the myth of the fish called Fishroe (Kun) which is thousands of miles large. It changes into a bird with a wingspan measuring thousands of miles across called the Friendlybird (Peng). When Friendlybird flies, it rises three thousand miles up in the sky and it looks like clouds. As it flies it churns up the waters of the ocean for a thousand miles. It can soar for six months without resting. When it gazes down at the human world, earthly figures look like specks of dust so that a crowd of humans appears the same as a herd of wild animals.

The most majestic and lyrical narrative of metamorphosis is the myth of the semi-divine first human being named Coiled Antiquity (Pan Gu). As this giant lay dying, his human form was divinely transformed into the parts of the cosmos. His breath became the wind and clouds, his eyes became the sun and moon, his bodily fluids became rivers and rains, and his flesh the soil. From the insects on his dying body were born the first human beings, who were called 'the black-haired people', an ancient name for the Chinese people.

Metamorphosis occurs also in the myth of the primeval goddess Woman Gua. First it is told that she made seventy transformations and created all things in the world. It is also told that her guts were divinely changed and became the composite deity of ten gods called the Guts of Woman Gua. Her power was so great that her bodily parts retained their divine nature and were immortalized in another form.

There is often a symbolic relationship between the deity or mythical figure who is transformed and the newly metamorphosed state. For example, the criminals who murdered a god turned into rapacious birds of evil omen, the osprey and the kite. Similarly, the maple trees into which the god of war's fetters changed symbolize bloodshed through their brilliant red foliage. The toad into which the moon goddess changed was believed to represent regeneration because it sloughs off its old skin and appears to be reborn. In Chinese mythology the state of immortality means the state of eternal youth, and that is what the moon goddess achieved when she ate some of her consort's stolen elixir. Moreover, the moon of which she became a goddess is also a symbol of regeneration because of its cyclical waxing and waning, which appears to be a cycle of birth, full life and death, and then rebirth. The hollow mulberry trunk into which the mother of Officer Govern (Yi Yin) turned is a symbol of the womb, and the river that the mother-mulberry log floated on is an emblem of life and the waters of birth. Her son grew up and became the hero who was a loyal minister of the mythical Shang king, Tang the Conqueror.

The theme of punishment appears in many stories of metamorphosis. The god of war was punished for challenging the Great God Yellow, and Hugefish was executed for the sacrilege of theft, the same crime for which the moon goddess was turned into an ugly if immortal toad. The transformed states of Cinnabar Crimson, Awe Osprey, Mount Drum, Sprite Guard and King Watch in avian myth all fit this pattern of punitive metamorphosis.

Fabled flora and fauna

Stories relating to nature myth are an early form of unnatural natural history. The mythical bestiary and vegetal myths include divine creatures and plants that express concepts of primitive allegory. The real or imaginary features of animals and plants are shown to possess moral significance. For example, it is related that a mythical judge called Esteemed Potter (Gao Yao), whose complexion was like a peeled melon and who had a horse's muzzle, owned a sacred ram with one horn. When the judge was hearing a case, he would order his ram to butt the guilty person. The innocent were never butted by the divine creature. In the same way three marvellous plants helped the ideal ruler Lofty (Yao) during his administration of the first human government. One plant grew a new petal each day for fifteen days and then shed one petal for the next fifteen days, so that it served Lofty as a natural calendar. Another plant could not only predict an omen, but when it was placed in a hot kitchen it could cool the air by fanning its huge leaves. The third plant possessed the power of knowing who was a flatterer. When a flatterer came to Lofty's court, the plant would bend towards the imposter and point him out. It was called the Point-the-Flatterer plant.

The fabulous calendar plant of Lofty (Yao), the ideal ruler.

Great Meet (Tai Feng), the god of luck.

The most valuable source of bestial and vegetal myths is the *Classic of Mountains and Seas*. Many myths relate to birds of omen, such as the bird like a cock with a human face whose song calls its own name, 'Fu-shee!' When it appears war will break out. Another relates to a mountain animal that looks human but is covered with pig's bristles. It lives in a cave and makes a sound like chopped wood. When it appears this is an omen of military conscription.

This classic is also a valuable source for descriptions of deities. They are depicted in a great variety of ways, with pig's ears, antlers, a reptilian body, a monkey's snout, wings, horns, a bovine body, tiger claws, panther tail, and human-faced or owl-faced. Many deities are represented as hybrid beings having the physical attributes of several real or imaginary creatures. The god of chaos, Muddle Thick (Hundun), for example, has a pig-like body, feline paws and four wings, but no head or face. The god of luck, Great Meet (Tai Feng), has a human shape but is covered in fur and has a tiger's tail. The divine minister of the rebel god Common Work has a snake's body and nine human heads. The deity called Land My (Lu Wu) has the body of a tiger with nine tails, feline claws and nine human heads. The deity Sky God (Tian Shen) looks like an ox; it has eight feet, two heads and a horse's tail, and it drones

The god Land My (Lu Wu).

The god Mount Drum (Gu Shan).

like a beetle. When this god appears it is an omen of war. The god Mount Drum (Gu Shan) has a dragon's body and a human face. But after it was hacked to death in retribution for the murder of another god, it changed into a kite-like mountain pheasant with scarlet and yellow markings. When it appears this is an omen of severe drought.

The potency of these and other deities is manifested in their domination and control of the natural world and the elements. They preside over mountains and rivers, and they make their appearance known by a flash of light or a rumbling sound like thunder. Many deities are generative, and they produce fields, fertile soil and bumper harvests. They also create sunlight and rain, without which plants cannot grow. The deity Torch Shade (Zhu Yin), who lives on Mount Bell, is a calendrical figure. When his eyes open it is daylight, and when they shut darkness falls. When he blows it is winter, and when he calls out it is summer. This deity never drinks, eats or breathes, but if he does breathe there are severe gales. He is portrayed with a scarlet serpentine body which is over three hundred miles long, and he has a human face.

Emblems and attributes

Mythical creatures serve as divine emblems. Three bluebirds and felines are emblems of the goddess of plague and punishment, Queen Mother of the West, who is herself depicted with the features of a tigress and a panther's tail. Her later emblem was the nine-tailed fox. Other emblematic animals are the ram of divine intelligence associated with the mythical judge Gao Yao, the soulful nightjar of the exiled King Watch, the bear associated with the myths of Hugefish (Gun) and Reptilian-Pawprint (Yu), and the toad and hare

The nine-tailed fox, a divine emblem of the Queen Mother of the West.

with the moon goddess Ever Sublime (Chang E).

Other natural emblems are linked to the myths of certain deities, such as millet with the grain deity Sovereign Millet, red maple with Jest Much the god of war, the owl and turtle with the failed flood-queller Hugefish (Gun), and the divine avenger and bringer of rain Responding Dragon with the Great God Yellow. Snakes of different colours are the attribute of many deities. They are held in the hand, trodden underfoot, worn in the ears or on the head, and chewed by deities and mythical beings. Snakes also have the function of guarding the tombs of deities and heroes who have changed into another form.

Responding Dragon (Ying Long), divine avenger and bringer of rain.

The world tree

The myth of the world tree is narrated in several passages of classical texts. The world tree is represented as an *axis mundi*, that is, the point where the sky and the earth meet in a vision of the perfect centre of the cosmos. The Building Tree (Jian Mu) is said to grow at the centre of the world, and it casts no shadow and releases no echo. It has green leaves, a purple trunk, black blossom and yellow fruit. It grows a thousand feet high without bearing branches, and then at its crown its branches grow into nine tanglewoods, while its roots form nine intertwining knots. Another world tree described in mythic narratives is the giant Peach Tree (Da Tao Mu) which forms a ladder to the sky. On its crown are celestial gates guarded by stern gods of punishment with their ferocious beasts who banish evil mortals trying to enter paradise. There are also the Trinity Mulberry Tree, the Seeker Tree, Accord Tree and Leaning Mulberry, which all form an *axis mundi*.

Leaning Mulberry (Fu Sang) is the most important of these mythological trees. It grows in the east and stands near Boiling Water Valley (in a variant, Warm Springs Valley). Its trunk is described as being a hundred miles

Leaning Mulberry (Fu Sang), the world tree, bearing the ten suns in its branches. Each new sun is carried to the crown of the tree by a bird in this detail of a unique funerary silk painting from Mawangdui.

high. It has the unique function of bearing the ten suns in its branches after each disc has journeyed through the sky and been rinsed and purified by its sun-mother, Breath Blend (Xi He). When the new sun for the day has been dried and revitalized, it is carried to the crown of Leaning Mulberry by a bird before it departs for its worldly passage.

The world mountain

Another form of the *axis mundi* is the world mountain. The most celebrated is the mountain range of Kunlun in the west. One of its peaks is the home of deities descending from heaven. The peak called Mount Jade (in a variant, Mount Flamingfire) is the kingdom of Queen Mother of the West. The world mountain range of Kunlun is also visited by shamans who make their ascent to the sky from its vertiginous summit and who gather the herbs of immortality from its highest slopes. This earthly paradise is full of mythical animals and plants. It is guarded by the feline beast Openbright (Kai-ming), which has nine heads with human faces that all face the east. There are also serpents, a dragon, ferocious felines and birds of prey, such as the six-headed hawk. The divine creature the Lookflesh (Shi Rou) lives there. It is a mass of flesh like an ox's liver with two eyes. When it has been eaten it grows again into the same shape. Three birds of paradise watch over Kunlun's paradise. They wear a serpent on their heads and tread a snake underfoot, and they have a scarlet snake on their breasts. They also wear armour on their heads. There are twelve marvellous trees on Kunlun, such as the Neverdie Tree of immortality, the precious Jade Tree that is guarded by a three-headed man, the Wise Man tree and the Sweet Water tree. It was on this mountain paradise that six shamans tended the corpse of the murdered god Notch Flaw and held the drug of immortality over him to revive him.

The world mountain has an important function in cosmology. In one of the Chinese creation myths the world picture is represented as a domed sky fastened to the flat earth by vast mountains, four in all. One of them, Mount Not Round, features in the catastrophe myth of the marplot Common Work. He rebelled against the power of the sky god, fought with him for supremacy and butted against the prop supporting the sky in the north, Mount Not Round. Other names for these sky props are Mount Notroundborechild, Mount Notstraight and Mount Notwhole. Their significance is not so much as an *axis mundi*, but as natural rocky blocks which keep the sky separate from the earth and so maintain the primeval process of creation.

Besides the earthly paradise of Kunlun in the mountainous west there are other utopian landscapes in descriptive mythic narratives, which are full of mythic flora and fauna. The sites of the burial places of gods and heroes are utopias. They are represented with typical mythic motifs, such as the cosmic number nine signifying the divine sky and the colour scarlet which is the emblem of life-giving power. Utopian motifs include idealized concepts of gigantic size, infinite space and vast distances. These representations create vivid pictorial images of the celestial archetype.

Strange lands and peoples

The inspiration for early Chinese writings on geography was the myth of Reptilian-Pawprint (Yu) and the flood. Some narratives describe his progress through the mythological world known as the Nine Provinces within the Four Seas. According to these accounts, as he travelled over rivers and mountains in his task of controlling the flood, he charted the land and listed the names of local tribes and customs. Early Chinese books mention numerous peoples living near the borders of the territory of the first Shang state, and then that of the Zhou, and also the greater political entity of the Han empire, the three dynasties covering the period between *c.* 1700 BC and AD 200. These peoples just beyond the borders were non-Chinese ethnic groups. They included the Tibeto-Burman Qiang of the north-west, who were probably related to the ancient Rong people from whom the Zhou evolved, and the Miao-Yao along the Yangtze River, including the Ba of Sichuan and the Man tribe of Hunan. The Tai were from the deep south, and the Yi were part of an Austro-Asiatic language group of east China. The Di were a northern people, and the Xiongnu of the north may have been linked to the ancient Scythians.

It was in the Han dynasty, around 100 BC, that the first official Chinese envoys went to foreign lands and recorded their experiences. These accounts were incorporated into the earliest historical records. Han historians maintained a reasonably unbiased viewpoint when they wrote of the customs, appearance, language and names of foreign peoples.

But travel writers of an imaginative mind set down quite different accounts of the peoples they encountered or heard of beyond the pale of Chinese civilization. Their impressions belong to mythology rather than history. They viewed foreigners negatively and often chose abusive characters or graphs with which to represent the names of foreign peoples, suggesting they were bestial or deformed. Foreigners were seen as oddly coloured, misshapen people, and this mythological expression is reflected in the names of their countries. For example, writers invented the names of Forkedtongue, Threehead, Hairy Folk, White Folk, Loppyears, Nogut, One-eyed, Oddarm and Onefoot.

But these mythological depictions may sometimes contain useful socio-logical data about an unfamiliar tribe. Names which indicate a physical deformity such as One-eyed may be explained by the social practice of inflict-ing mutilation as a punishment or as a means of tribal identification. The name Forkedtongue suggests the practice of slitting the tongue in the initia-tion rite of a shaman. Other names, such as Deepseteyes or White Folk, describe non-Chinese features. Peoples described as having two heads or dual bodies may refer to what we know as Siamese twins.

While negative representations convey deep-seated anxieties on the part of classical authors about the nature of the Chinese self in relation to the cul-tural 'other', many narratives about foreign peoples also seek to explain their origin and customs through the medium of myth. For example, there is the myth of how Piercedchest Country acquired its physical characteristic and its name. It relates that when the semi-divine Reptilian-Pawprint (Yu) convened the first assembly of the gods, one deity arrived late, so he slew him. But when he went on to control the world flood, he came to the land of the slain deity where two of the dead god's officers attacked Reptilian-Pawprint in revenge and pierced him. But he was lifted up into the sky by two dragons. The two officers realized that he had been saved by a miracle and that he was a god, so they stabbed themselves in the heart from remorse. But Reptilian-Pawprint took pity on them and revived them with the drug of immortality. Ever afterwards this people bore the mark of this episode in the form of a hole or hollow in the chest.

The myth of Oddarm Country bears the mark of a migration myth. It is told that the people of this country have only one arm, but they have three eyes which serve for daylight and darkness. They ride on piebald horses with a two-headed, brightly coloured bird perched beside them. They are good fowlers and are ingenious at finding ways to carry difficult loads on their shoulders. These people are also inventors. One of their most famous inven-

People of Piercedchest Country.

*A traveller from
Oddarm Country.*

tions was a flying machine which used the currents of the wind. It is told that once a west wind blew their flying machines into Shang territory in the reign of Tang the Conqueror. The king feared their invention and destroyed their machines so that his people would not know about this means of travel. Later the Oddarm travellers made more flying machines and in the end the king allowed them to return home on them.

Ornithological narratives are frequent in the repertoire of Chinese myths. They tell of the Feathered Folk (Yu Min) who are hatched from eggs and are born with feathers. They are said to have a bird's beak, scarlet eyes and a white head. Several myths tell how divine birds taught humans how to survive by eating bird's eggs. The myth of human–avian hybrids called the Chief Xi (Meng Xi) relates mythic themes of the domestication of animals, of eating (sitiogony) and migration. The people of Chief Xi have a human head and a bird's body. In the beginning of their story, their founders tamed and domesticated all birds and beasts and were the first to eat eggs. When the people wanted to migrate to a better land, divine birds led them to the land of Chief Xi and showed them where to settle in the mountains, which had a plentiful supply of magnificent bamboos eight thousand feet high. The divine birds also showed them how to eat parts of the bamboo, and the people made that place their country.

The myth of the Country of Women embodies myths of gender competition, gender roles, matriarchy, virgin birth and the fertilizing power of bathing. As we have seen, it is told that the Country of Women lies north of the land of a shaman who knew the secret art of reviving a corpse. Their country was surrounded by water and beside a yellow pool. When the women bathe in this pool they become pregnant. If their child is male, the mothers do not nurture it and let it die before it reaches the age of three. Only female babies are allowed to survive. The mythic motif of the fertilizing bathe is evident also in the origin myth of the ancestress of the Shang dynasty. The motif of the colour yellow also occurs in the myth of the creation of humankind by the goddess Woman Gua who made humans out of yellow clay.

The most valuable source for myths of foreign countries and peoples is the *Classic of Mountains and Seas*. The last chapters of that book relate numerous genealogical myths, which tell how various deities gave birth to tribes and peoples and founded countries for them. For example, the Great God Foremost founded Blacktooth Country in the east, and a deity called Loppy Ears gave his name to his descendants in their own country. The hero

Reptilian-Pawprint (Yu) is said to have brought about the creation of the Hairy Folk. When one of his descendants killed a deity called Tender Human, a great god took pity on the people of Tender Human and created a country for them, and they became the Hairy Folk.

Chinese geography gradually became less mythological and more of a scientific study as speculation about the old world of gods, goddesses and heroic figures gave way to a real knowledge of the new Chinese empire of the Han and its neighbouring lands and peoples. Despite this, myths which emphasized the difference between Chinese and foreign peoples took root in the national consciousness and have endured for two millennia. These myths established the idea of a cultural hierarchy in which China enjoyed a superior status, while other countries either were given grudging approval or were relegated to the nadir of barbarism.

Continuities in the
mythic tradition

Chinese writers and scholars through the centuries transmitted the mythological repertoire in much the same form as it had first been recorded in antiquity. That is, the classical books which contained the mythic narratives were preserved for the most part, and so the myths became part of the written record. That they were preserved is mainly due to Chinese scholarly reverence for the sacred canon of antiquity. Yet no individual writer or editor felt inspired to gather the mythological passages from the books of the classics and shape them into an artistic whole.

That mythic texts were preserved does not mean they stagnated once they had entered the canon and later were printed in the first published books of around AD 1000. Nor does it mean that classical myths experienced no outward change. On the contrary, later writers influenced myth in two major ways. Some writers transmitted myth by quoting it in their works, while at the same time interpreting the myth in a completely different sense from its original meaning, altering myth according to the spirit of the customs and values of their own times. This is particularly evident in the case of the first author to write a commentary to the ancient *Classic of Mountains and Seas*. He was Guo Pu (276–324), a learned scholar and a poet who was influenced by the new vogue of mysticism and alchemy in the early fourth century. He was separated from the earliest myths recorded in the classic by at least five hundred years. By his time, the old myths were no longer believed and often were not even understood. In trying to interpret them, Guo sometimes changed their basic meaning.

Other writers consciously rejected the content and meaning of the myths of antiquity and wrote critical works with the intention of disproving the acts of the gods and the superhuman feats of past heroes. The late classical writer Wang Chong (27–100) was such an author. In his essays he goes to great lengths to prove that mythic events could not have occurred. To the modern reader his arguments sometimes sound comical, since Wang supported them with occasional superstitious beliefs which are now self-evidently mistaken. Nevertheless, despite the bias and incomprehension of such authors, they preserved the myths, which became a valued part of the cultural tradition.

Although in one sense a mythic narrative becomes fixed once it is written down, it remains a flexible force in the sacred beliefs of a nation. The potency of ancient myth is expressed in many forms of Chinese culture – the arts, religion, state ritual, education, social mores, historical writing, in politics, and in the expression of national identity.

The clearest example of this is seen in literature. The nature poet Tao Yuanming (365–427) lived a little later than the interpreter of myth Guo Pu. Guo had access to a set of illustrations to the myths recorded in the *Classic of Mountains and Seas*, and he wrote a set of verses on them. Tao Yuanming wrote a famous series of thirteen poems called 'On Reading the *Classic of Mountains and Seas*', in which he described his reaction to reading the old book and looking at the illustrations to it in the form of a narrative scroll. The myths that Tao singles out for admiration are about Boast Father who raced with the sun, the doomed bird Sprite Guard who was transformed from the goddess Woman Lovely, and the warrior Heaven Punished who carried on fighting even when he had been decapitated. An interesting feature of Tao's selection of myths is that most of his figures were heroic failures. The poet was himself writing in a time of political unrest, when the Chinese court had been driven out of the ancestral heartland of the Central Plains and forced into exile south of the Yangtze River. The message the poet conveyed through his use of these myths is that it does not matter whether one wins or loses so long as one has high aspirations and is dedicated to one's cause.

The Tang poet Li He (790–816) wrote within the mythological tradition, conjuring up visions of goddesses, shamans and mystical figures. He also lived in a period of unrest, when the Tang empire (618–906) was threatened by rebellious militia. His creative spirit was revitalized by the divine world of antiquity. He describes, for example, Mount Wu with the line, 'Its emerald rocky clusters pierce high heaven', evoking the numinous haunt of goddesses and female shamans of the old culture of the Yangtze River.

The stellar myth of the unhappy love of Weaver Woman and Oxherd became a popular theme in love poetry during the Period of Disunity between the Han and the Tang (220–618). Southern poets in exile focused on the mythical figure of Weaver Woman as she waits for her one night of love and fulfilment on the Seventh Night of the Seventh Month. Her frustrated desire may be read as an allegory of political disenchantment among Southern courtier poets who longed for a return to their ancestral heartland in the north.

The myth of the goddess of the northern Luo River is commemorated in literature and in art. First represented in a rhapsody by the royal poet Cao Zhi (192–232), the river goddess is a capricious and flirtatious figure who denies the amorous desire of mortal men. Later, the painter Gu Kaizhi (*c.* 344–406) painted a famous narrative silk scroll telling of the doomed love between the prince and the goddess. This artistic evocation of the river goddess is based on mythic fragments, such as that presented by an early com-

Goddess of the Luo River as painted on a handscroll in the 12th century, based on the style of Gu Kaizhi (c. 344–c. 406).

mentator who related that the hunter god Yi the Archer dreamed that he had an affair with this goddess, named Fu Fei, the spirit of Luo River.

A unique silk painting has recently been discovered in the tomb of a noblewoman known as Lady Dai (Xin Chui) who died *c.* 168 BC. The site is south of the Yangtze River, at Mawangdui near Changsha in Hunan province. It is a narrative painting which tells the story of the dead woman's journey from the human world of her funeral to her eternal life in the western mountain paradise. The climax of the picture shows her immortal soul in her human form, complete with her walking stick, asking the way to the gates of heaven. Beyond the gates are the world tree of the east, with nine of its daily suns hanging out to dry, and the crescent moon in the western sky with its hare and toad and the moon goddess Ever Sublime (Chang E). The figure of a goddess reigns supreme over the cosmos, represented in the painting on three planes: a watery underworld, the human world on earth and the celestial sphere. The goddess is depicted with a serpentine tail and long flowing hair, and she glows with a divine crimson light. Around her the birds of paradise sing in heavenly harmony. The anonymous painter of this superb

Funerary silk painting from the early Han dynasty tomb of Lady Dai (Xin Chui) at Mawangdui. It relates a narrative of nine episodes (see p. 68).

EPISODE 9
(left) Above the crescent moon are the hare and toad, holding the drug of immortality. Below is the figure of a young girl, either the moon goddess or the immortalized Lady Dai.
(centre below) The bell of destiny.

EPISODE 8
Guardians of the Gates of Heaven.

EPISODE 6
Either the owl, symbol of death, or the bat, symbol of happiness.

EPISODE 4
Feline beasts guard the sacred chart of the skies.

EPISODE 2
The human world, showing the funeral feast of Lady Dai.

Diagram of the narrative episodes in the funerary silk painting (see p. 67).

EPISODE 9
(centre top) Serpentine female deity, sovereign of t cosmos. Belo her, two bird collect the aroma from t cooked funer feast.
(right) The rising sun, wi symbolic bird at the top of the world tre which holds t other suns.

EPISODE 7
The canopy c the sky with two divine birds.

EPISODE 5
Lady Dai asks the way to paradise, accompanied by her three ladies-in-waiting.

EPISODE 3
The aerial sphere, symboliz by the round jade (*bi*).

EPISODE 1
The watery underworld where the mortal soul will perish; a giant holds the fl surface of the earth.

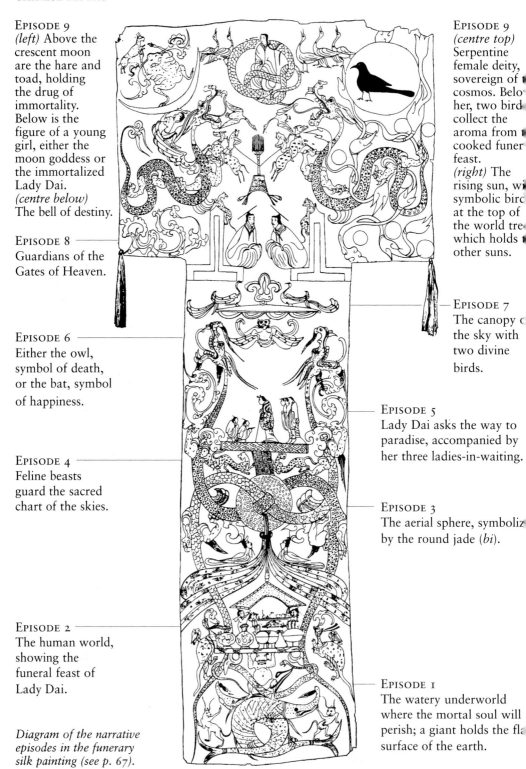

silk funeral banner has made creative use of early myth to depict the dead woman's rite of passage to paradise. For example, the figure wafted up to the moon appears to be the moon goddess, but she might also suggest the rejuvenated figure of Lady Dai as she was as a young girl. The presiding goddess at the centre of the picture appears to be the powerful creator deity Woman Gua, but she might also be Queen Mother of the West as she looks in welcome at the direction of the female figure ascending to the clouds around the moon. Since it was the custom in traditional China for tombs, coffins and funereal objects to be prepared before the death of the occupant of the tomb, it is likely that Lady Dai watched the painting taking shape and directed the painter to represent her favourite mythic stories on the banner that was eventually laid to rest on her coffin.

The ethnic myths contained in the *Classic of Mountains and Seas* originally expressed Chinese fears of the unknown lands and peoples beyond their borders. The structure of the classic is based on a mythological journey around China and to all its outlying regions in the four cardinal directions. This structure and the plot of visiting strange countries and peoples were inventively used by a late-eighteenth-century novelist named Li Ruzhen (1763–c. 1830). He translated the ancient myths into an original and amusing novel in which he satirized not foreigners but his own Chinese people. His novel, *Flowers in the Mirror*, tells how the hero travels around imaginary countries with similar or the same names as those in the ancient classic. In describing grotesque customs, manners and appearance among various peoples the hero meets, the author criticizes some of the negative national characteristics of China as he saw them, such as hypocrisy in the Country of Two-faced People, greed in the Country of Long-armed People, and excessive seriousness in the Country of Scholars. He used the Country of Women to denounce the Chinese custom of footbinding, presenting the women of that country as men and vice versa, so that it is the men who have to endure the agony of having their feet squashed into the sexually attractive shape of

The result of footbinding was a shape called the 'Golden Lotus'.

69

The Monkey King (Mei Hou Wang), the most familiar figure in Chinese opera.

'Golden Lotuses'. Li's reversal of gender roles was effective social satire and a fine example of the enduring power of myth to challenge traditional customs and beliefs.

Myths of divine creatures and animalian deities are vividly transmitted in Chinese culture through art and the performing arts. The most familiar figure is that of the Monkey King (Mei Hou Wang) in Chinese opera. The opera of the *Monkey King* was itself based on the sixteenth-century novel *Journey to the West*, attributed to Wu Chengen (*c.* 1506–82). The novel tells the story of a monk's pilgrimage from China to India to collect Buddhist scriptures. He is accompanied by Monkey, the main character of the novel, who is known as 'The Monkey Who is Enlightened about the State of Emptiness', and also by Pig, Sand Monk and White Horse. The opera focuses on Monkey's divine playfulness and his godlike power of metamorphosis and magical travel.

The flood myths of the classics became less important in the modern era than the stories of the world flood that were preserved in the oral traditions of minority groups in south China. Forty-nine versions of this minority flood tradition exist, which all follow a similar plot. Their myth tells of a world flood in which the human race perished except for a brother and his sister, who survived by getting into a giant gourd which floated on the surging waters. When the flood subsided the gourd came to rest on land. The couple went on to marry and found a new race of humans. The theme of sibling marriage occurs also in one of the late myths of the foundation of the institution of marriage which features an unnamed brother and his sister Woman Gua. It is not known how old the minority flood myth is, since it was recorded in writing only in the twentieth century. It is representative of the many myths of ethnic peoples absorbed into the Chinese political system over the centuries which have co-existed with the more orthodox myths of the educated elite.

Some myths became perpetuated through the potent symbolism of historical personages. For example, the tomb of the great sky god Young

The tomb of the sky god, Young Brightsky (Shao Hao).

Brightsky (Shao Hao) is located near the modern shrine to Confucius (c. 551–479 BC) at Qufu in Shandong province, near the shrine to Mencius. In the flexible way of myth, the god's tomb is placed in the east although he was an ancient god of the west.

One of the primary teachings of the Confucian school of moral philosophy was the precept of filial piety. This family ethic was first dramatized by Mencius (c. 372–c. 289 BC) in the retelling of the myth of the three trials of Hibiscus (Shun) the dutiful son. Later, passages extolling the virtue of filial piety were gathered together and produced as the book, the *Classic of Filial*

The modern shrine to Confucius.

Piety. It became a basic text for the elementary education of boys, not only in China but throughout East Asia. Its most famous teaching that is still observed in the region states, 'The greatest rule of filial piety is to honour one's parents. The second is not to disgrace one's parents.' The archaic myth of filial Hibiscus (Shun) was preserved through the writings of Mencius, encapsulated in the precept of filial piety, incorporated into the Confucian classics, and revitalized through the writings of the famous medieval scholar Zhu Xi (1130–1200) and the late medieval philosopher Wang Yangming (1472–1529).

The flexibility and vitality of myth are seen in the way the precept of filial piety was adopted by the Taiping rebels in their revolutionary ideology in the nineteenth century. Although the xenophobic and anarchic followers of their leader, Hong Xinquan, destroyed images and temples dedicated to Confucian, Daoist and Buddhist deities and worthies, they honoured as their second moral precept (after a reverence for God, Jesus and their leader Hong) the ancient ideal of filial piety. The movement began as a violent ethnic revolt against the Manchus who had conquered China with their superior military power in 1644. The rebellion took root in the south-east and centred on the Hakka ethnic group of south China. It burnt itself out in the lower Yangtze region and was finally put down in 1860.

One of the major ways myth is perpetuated is through ritual. This process is exemplified in the magnificent imperial rite to the Altar of Heaven which began in the Han dynasty and continued into the early twentieth century. The late imperial celebration of this rite took place at the Temple of Heaven, a four-mile-square religious complex south-east of the Imperial Palace in Beijing. The temple consists of three buildings set in wooded grounds, the Altar of Heaven, the Imperial Vault of Heaven and the Hall of Prayer for Good Harvests. The rite of worship of Heaven took place at dusk on the eve of the winter solstice in December. The emperor was the celebrant as the priestly king. Clothed in the twelve-symbol dragon robe of embroidered golden silk, the emperor was carried in silence on a golden throne among a retinue of two thousand males along a yellow path symbolizing the earth. At dawn, to the sound of sacred music, he went up the three round white terraces of the Altar of Heaven, symbolizing the round dome of the sky, and worshipped the sky as his predecessors had done for two thousand years. The emperor's robe was decorated with twelve sacrificial emblems: the cosmic emblems of the sun and moon on the shoulders, the stars on the chest; and the world mountain, dragon and pheasant, the symbol of excellence, the

Part of the complex of the Temple of Heaven in Beijing.

Detail of a twelve-emblem imperial dragon robe of embroidered golden silk.

punitive axe-head symbolizing justice, as well as waterweed, two chalices, fire and grains of rice, were embroidered on the body of the robe. Most of these were emblems that originated in the Han dynasty.

The mythic symbolism of the earth, the archaic idea of the four-sided world of humans beneath the sacred cupola of the sky, has remained deeply embedded in the Chinese cultural consciousness. This mythic square of earth represented China in antiquity. As people in ancient China came to learn of other countries and peoples on their borders, so Chinese writers began to develop the idea of this mythic space that was their land as surrounded by four seas and four outer wildernesses bounded by the ends of the earth. This central mythic space they called 'The Central Kingdom' or 'The Middle Kingdom'. To them this space, the Middle Kingdom (Zhong Guo), was the universe, the real world, and everything that lay outside it was beyond the pale of civilization. For the sixty million Chinese living outside China today, in other parts of Asia and in Europe and America, the idea of the homeland that is the centre of the universe is an immense source of pride, and it is one that irresistibly draws them to 'return' (*gui*), to go home to die when their lives are drawing to an end.

Resonating through Chinese culture from antiquity to the twentieth century is the powerful mythical symbolism of the Golden Age of the ideal rulers Lofty (Yao), Hibiscus (Shun) and Reptilian-Pawprint (Yu). It is manifested in politics and history. Early in China's political history the myth of

Lofty (Yao). The inscription reads: 'The God Yao, Fang Hsun, was humane like Heaven itself, and wise like a divine being; to be near him was like approaching the sun, to look at him was like gazing into clouds'.

Hibiscus (Shun). The inscription reads: 'The God Shun, Chung Hua, ploughed beyond Mount Li; in three years he had developed it'.

Lofty's abdication in favour of his unrelated worthy minister Hibiscus, passing over his hereditary son, was exploited by successful military leaders who challenged the legitimate dynasty. To war lords such as General Cao Cao (d. AD 220), the Lofty abdication myth signified the supremacy of the political doctrine of abdication over hereditary succession, even if 'abdication' in fact meant the removal of the rightful emperor from the throne by force. General Cao Cao was a usurper, and his model of appropriating the throne from the Han emperor who 'abdicated' was one that later usurpers adopted as a political and legal precedent.

The myth of the Golden Age of Lofty, Hibiscus and Reptilian-Pawprint was also appropriated by China's first historian, Sima Qian (*c*. 145–*c*. 86 BC), who traced in his *Records of the Grand Historian* the beginnings of Chinese civilization from the Age of the Gods to the Golden Age of the Ideal Rulers. So potent was his reworking of the ancient myth that the archetype of the Golden Age of the Ideal Rulers became the archetype of the first human government. For centuries thereafter historians transformed the mythical figures of Lofty, Hibiscus and Reptilian-Pawprint into real historical personages who stood at the fountainhead of Chinese culture and civilization. This archetype has endured into the modern era. Its mythological inspiration rather than its historical authenticity reflects the power of myth to affirm and re-enact the sacred history of a nation.

Suggestions for further reading

Birrell, Anne. *Chinese Mythology: An Introduction.* (1993) Baltimore,
Johns Hopkins University Press, 1999.

Birrell, Anne. *The Classic of Mountains and Seas.* Penguin Classics.
London: Penguin Books, 1999.

De Bary, William Theodore, Wing-tsit Chan and Burton Watson, eds.
Sources of Chinese Tradition. 2 vols. Introduction to Oriental
Civilizations. New York and London: Columbia University Press,
1964.

Hawkes, David. *The Songs of the South: An Anthology of Ancient Chinese
Poems by Qu Yuan and Other Poets.* (1959). rev. edn. Penguin
Classics. Harmondsworth: Penguin Books, 1985.

Karlgren, Bernhard. *The Book of Odes.* Stockholm: Museum of Far
Eastern Antiquities, 1974 (poem nos 245 and 303).

Keightley, David N., ed. *The Origin of Chinese Civilization.* Studies on
China, 1. Berkeley, Los Angeles and London: University of California
Press, 1983.

Rawson, Jessica. *Ancient China: Art and Archaeology.* London: British
Museum Publications, 1980.

Watson, Burton. *The Complete Works of Chuang Tzu.* New York:
Columbia University Press, 1968.

Watson, Burton. *Records of the Grand Historian of China.* Translated
from the *Shih chi of Ssu-ma Ch'ien* [*Shi ji*, Sima Qian], 2 vols. New
York: Columbia University Press, 1961.

Wu Hung. *The Wu Liang Shrine.* Stanford: Stanford University Press,
1989.

Picture credits

The author and publisher acknowledge with thanks permission granted to reproduce the following illustrations including those previously published or printed elsewhere. Every effort has been made to trace copyright holders, but if any have been inadvertently overlooked, the publisher will be pleased to make the necessary arrangement at the first opportunity.

p. 6: John Gilkes; *pp. 7, 16, 27, 33, 38, 46, 51, 54, 60, 64:* adapted from Noel Barnard, *Studies on the Ch'u Silk Manuscript,* 2 vols, Canberra: Australian National University, Dept of Far Eastern History, 1973, vol. 1, pp. 2–3; *pp. 9, 10, 66:* © The British Museum (OA 1947.7-12.413; 1936.11-18.2; 1930.10-15.02 Add71); *p. 11:* adapted from Edwin O. Reischauer and John K. Fairbank, *East Asia: The Great Tradition,* 2 vols, Boston: Houghton Mifflin, 1960, vol. 1, p. 46; *pp. 13, 16, 21, 22, 23, 30, 34, 36, 44, 54, 75:* after Feng Yunpeng and Feng Yunyuan, *Shi suo [Research on Stone Carvings],* Part 2, *Jin Shi suo [Research on Bronze and Stone Carvings],* 12 *ch.,* 1821, reprinted Shanghai: Shangwu, 1934, by permission of the Syndics of Cambridge University Library; *pp. 17, 43, 45, 55, 56, 57:* after Hu Wen-huan, ed. (1596), *Shan hai jing tu [Illustrations to the Classic of Mountains and Seas],* photolithic reprint of the Ming edn of Hu, 1596, in the series Zhongguo gudai banhua zong, Shanghai: Guji, 1944, by permission of the Syndics of Cambridge University Library; *p. 18:* after Yuan Ke, *Shen hua xuan yi bai ti [One Hundred Myths: An Anthology with Translations and Annotations],* Shanghai: Guji chubanshe, 1980, p. 2; *pp. 19, 39, 49:* after Yuan Ke, *Zhongguo shen hua chuanshuo cidian [Dictionary of Chinese Myths and Legends],* Shanghai: Cishu chubanshe, 1985, p. 20 and unnumbered front pages [16a, 20b]; *pp. 31, 61, 62:* after Yuan Ke, *Shan hai jing jiaozhu [Collated Notes to the Classic of Mountains and Seas],* Shanghai: Guji chubanshe, 1980, pp. 214, 195, 213; *pp. 47, 58, 67:* after Wenwu, eds, *Xi Han bohua [The Western Han Silk Painting],* Beijing: Wenwu, 1972, by permission of the Syndics of Cambridge University Library; *p. 48:* after Shi Yan, *Zhongguo diaosu shi tu lu [Record of Historical Chinese Carvings and Brick Illustrations],* in the series Zhongguo meishu shi tu lu congshu, Shanghai: Renmin meishu, 1983, vol. 1, p. 248, by permission of the Syndics of Cambridge University Library; *p. 68:* after An Zhimin, *Changsha xin faxian di Xi Han bohua shi tan [An investigation into the Western Han Silk Painting Recently Discovered at Changsha], Kaogu* 1 (1973), 43–53, p. 44 (narrative explanations by Anne Birrell); *p. 69:* after Howard S. Levy, *Chinese Footbinding: The History of a Curious Erotic Custom,* New York: Bell Publishing Co., 1967, ch. 4, p. 69; *p. 70:* after 'The Monkey King', National Chinese Opera Theater [Chung-hua min-kuo kuo-chü t'uan], First North American Tour Program, Taipei: National Chinese Opera Theater, 1973–4, back cover; *pp. 71–3:* CITS (China International Tourist Service); *p. 74:* after Jean Mailey, *The Manchu Dragon: Costumes of the Ch'ing Dynasty 1644–1912,* New York: The Metropolitan Museum of Art, 1981, p. 16.

Index